A Modern Day Saint

FATHER GABRIEL MEJIA

Scott Werner, MD

Health & Longevity, Inc.
157 E Riverside Dr., #3F
St. George, UT 84790

ISBN (paperback): 978-1-941420-28-7

1 2 3 4 5 6 21 20 19 18 17
1st edition, April 2017

Printed in the United States and Canada

Edited by Marilyn King, Ph.D. –
    www.BlueLotusEditing.com

Table of Contents

Introduction

I kissed Vicki goodbye, checked my bag and made it through the TSA security check without incident.

The flight to Denver was a bumpy ride with turbulence moving the plane up and down, right and left. After 50 minutes and with my stomach up in my throat, I finally asked the angels to smooth out the ride and protect us. Thank goodness, the jet became calm, almost eerily quiet, and we enjoyed the last 25 minutes of smooth sailing and made a perfect landing at Denver airport.

I had a 3-½ hour layover before my flight to Houston, so I walked to Wolfgang Puck, the restaurant with the best coffee at the Denver International Airport.

My thoughts kept going to the past eight months of meeting St. Germaine, learning about the 24-strand DNA manifestation and the evolution we humans are to go through to survive the physical toxicity of the planet from petrochemicals (herbicides and pesticides), radiation still spewing from Fukushima and Chernobyl, the new nanobot and artificial intelligence threat from human technology, and the emotional turmoil we continue to put on each other every day.

St Germaine had told me in October 2014 that I would be heading to Colombia, South America, in June 2015 to write another book about Padre Gabriel. "Who?" I had wondered, as at the time I hadn't started writing *The Next Step in Human Evolution.* In fact, I didn't have the time to write another book.

In 2012, I had flown to Honolulu to write my memoirs, but instead, due to angelic intervention, I had written *Take Back Your Health* which ended up being a great oracle book to help people get to the core causes of their diseases with herbal suggestions and emotional release techniques and other modalities to remove the blockages to energy flow.

Three years later, in January 2015, I flew off to Maui, where I experienced personal visitations by St. Germaine, who appeared with the information for *The Next Step in Human Evolution*, It was published on Earth Day, April 22, of 2015. One day before to my trip to Colombia, I received the first copies of *The Next Step in Human Evolution* in Spanish, just in time to take them with me to South America.

I am a Medical Intuitive. I see, hear, feel and know what is causing dis-ease within the human body. Remarkably, I also trained as a medical doctor at Saint Louis University Medical School graduating with the class of 1986, and completed a residency as an obstetrician/gynecologist at Good Samaritan Medical Center and passed the ACOG written Boards in June 1990. Because of my scientific mind and education, I know about the modern treatments of disease. Because of spirit and intuition, I can hone in on the real causes of our dis-ease, afflictions and suffering.

Most, if not all, disease begins in-utero with emotions and inherited DNA from parents, who propagate and pass on those emotions, quantum energy, genetics and chromosomes containing weakness, breakage and trauma. These cause us to be born with possibilities of disease and mental illness, which eventually will be treated in a modern day medical system with powerful chemicals created by the pharmaceutical industry, surgery and cosmetic treatments, psychoanalysis and psychotherapy.

The recurrence rate of these diseases is extremely high (greater than 90%) in the United States. I've been sent by St. Germaine to Colombia, South America, to investigate a system created with love therapy as the core principle of treatment. The system was created by Padre Gabriel Mejia of the Hogares Claret and incorporates the love and knowledge of many Masters including Viktor Frankl (Logotherapy), Maharishi (Transcendental Meditation) and Padre Gabriel Mejia himself, using principles of essential oils, flower essences, group therapy, companionship therapy, self-love and self worth, integration into peaceful society, exercise, recreation, and scouting. It is a system with a 98% success rate after 10 years of treating some of the most difficult emotional and behavioral crises affecting our world.

I have come on this adventure to find out about this system, what it is, and why it works so well.

So...three months after writing *The Next Step in Human Evolution*, I am in Medellín, Colombia, to write a new book about Padre Gabriel Antonio Mejia Montoya, a Catholic Claretian Priest, founder of Hogares Claret, and the marvelous work of reconstructing a country ravaged by the drug cartel wars of the late eighties into our current time.

Chapter 1 - Trip to the Compound

June 1, 2015

The flight out of Houston, Texas, was delayed for three hours. We were supposed to fly out just prior to midnight, but didn't end up boarding the plane till 2:30 AM. Luckily, I had a one-time pass to the United Club in Houston, so I was able to be in comfort for the four hours there.

Arriving in Bogotá three hours late, I had to get a different flight. The local Avianca Airlines was very helpful getting me tickets for the next flight to Medellín, but I had no phone coverage, even though I had made arrangements with Verizon for international phone usage. I had a South American cell phone, which I used in Peru two years ago, but I hadn't bought a SIM card for usage in Colombia yet, rendering it useless as well.

As I arrived into the Medellín Airport three hours late, I had no idea where I was going and I assumed the people who were to pick me up had already left. I picked up my bag at the baggage claim and headed out the exit to come up with a new plan.

A man standing near me could see my desperation. Knowing I needed help, he called me over in broken English, told me to follow him to a phone, then used his own money and attempted to call the only number I had, to Monica Tovar in Bucaramanga, a city half a country away in Colombia.

As this dear man was dialing, I heard a voice calling, "Doctor Scott." I quickly looked to my right, where a young, handsome Colombian man was moving toward me.

1

"Doctor Scott, I've been worried sick about you. I didn't have the right flight number."

Since my flight had been delayed by over three hours from Houston to Bogotá, Colombia, he still had the first flight number.

"Doctor Scott, Camilo Estrella is my name. I didn't have the right flight information for the plane."

I said, "Hi, I am Scott Werner, from Utah. My plane was delayed for 3 hours which made me miss my connection from Bogotá to Medellín." Camilo emotionally stated, "Padre Gabriel has been worried sick that something might have happened to you. I'm so glad that you are all right. Padre Gabriel told me to pick you up and bring you to the compound, where he is busy with meetings this morning. Please follow me," Camilo added, as he easily threw my 50-pound bag over his shoulder and started walking toward the parking lot.

I followed Camilo out into the fresh morning air of Palo Negro, where the larger airport of Medellín Antioquia had been constructed. There was no room for a large international airport in the valley where the city of Medellín was located as it had been filled to capacity with buildings and highways. We loaded my two bags into his older Ford Explorer and headed away from the airport, toward the mountain range to the northwest.

As the Ford Explorer groaned, climbing the steep pass up through the Andes Mountains and passing a summit with stunningly beautiful evergreens all around, Camilo was full of questions. Who was I? Why had I come to Colombia? How had I heard of Padre Gabriel? Had I met Maharishi? When did I learn about and was taught Transcendental Meditation?

Camilo continued his conversation in English and I started my own line of interrogation as we started winding down a steep, well-constructed road into the city of Medellín. How did Camilo learn to speak English? Answer: Attending Maharishi University of Management for 4 years. What was his focus? Answer: Ayurvedic Medicine and Panchakarma (cleansing the body and mind). We both became well acquainted in the 50 minutes as he drove down one of the many mountains, which surround Medellín. We slowly got into more traffic as we approached the beautiful city. Many small yellow cabs appeared on the road and motorcycles zoomed all around us.

After a drive of about 40 minutes, we started to go up a mountain on the other side of the valley, which was filled with beautiful high-rise buildings, many made of a reddish coral color, matching the smaller buildings around them. Finally, we came to a gated compound with a large, metal yellow gate. Camilo honked the horn and the gate began to open.

We entered a beautiful courtyard with many tropical plants and flowers. Two men dressed in white were busy working on a large, exotic swimming pool. Nearby was a shallow, smaller pool for children. The pools hadn't been filled with water yet, but already looked so inviting. Off to the left was a tall, white, three-story building, which looked like a small hotel. A longer, red brick building was to the right which, I learned later, had a large kitchen and dining area and a large game and meeting room.

I got out of the SUV and stared at my surroundings, which seemed very familiar. I walked behind the large red brick building and discovered six sinks and soaking areas, possibly for washing cloths, I thought. Above the soaking area and to the left of the building was a water-gathering tank of probably 1-2,000 gallons. The tank had two taps and even larger washing baths. Down below, to the north of the buildings and pools, a beautiful road made of brick led to an enclosed, large basketball/tennis court. A small stream flowed down the north side of the property from a fairly large pond, filled with ducks and lily pads, behind these two buildings.

Camilo called to me, "Padre Gabriel is anxious to meet with you. Let us go to the house!"

I had been so busy taking in the scenery of the compound, I hadn't noticed he was waiting for me, with my larger bag up on his shoulder. "Coming," I answered.

Chapter 2 - Meeting Padre Gabriel

We ascended along a concrete path by a large grass archery field. There were five foam targets, placed at various distances, and a large shed with chairs sitting underneath to give shade for the archers. The shed appeared to be thirty or forty years old.

As we walked, the path turned west around the field. I noticed trees had been growing for many years all the way around the perimeter of the land, with bushes interweaving in between the trees. A 12-14-foot-tall chain-link fence provided additional privacy around the entire compound, which I assessed to be approximately ten acres.

Following a path of rectangular stones with colorful flowering bushes on either side, we started ascending a fairly steep hill, heading to the main house of Los Tres Padres (The Three Fathers as I would call them), el Padre Gabriel Antonio Mejia Montoya, el Padre José and el Padre Orlando.

I could hear the voices of many men speaking in Spanish as I climbed the hill. A meeting of the leaders of the Hogares Claret was being held in two groups. A group of ten was on a large covered patio outside the house, where I was greeted by each individual with much pleasure. When we entered the house, there were twelve more men, meeting in a living room area about 20 x 12 feet in size.

Padre Gabriel stood up to greet me and said in Spanish, "Doctor Scott Werner, we have been so worried about you, and we are glad you are safely here in our house. Our house is your house for as long as you would like to stay." He was a charming older man dressed in a traditional tailored shirt of Latin America, who had such a kind face and smile. Padre Gabriel continued, "How was your flight? We didn't have the correct flight number and Camilo stayed at the airport just in case you came later. Can I see your ticket?"

I handed both tickets to Padre Gabriel. I told him I had to take a different flight, because the flight from Houston, Texas, was over three hours late arriving in Bogotá, Colombia, causing me to miss my earlier flight. His face took on a look of comprehension, and he gave me the first of many smiles to come. He nodded his head stating, "The missed flight was the flight number I had."

Padre Gabriel introduced me to everyone in the room and we all shook hands vigorously. All the men greeted me in Spanish. I answered back in Spanish, as best I could. Padre Gabriel showed me to my private room which was just off the front meeting area, through a doorway to the west side of the living area. It was about 12 x 12 feet in size, held a queen-sized bed with a colorful bedspread, and had an attached private bathroom and shower. Father Gabriel said, "Refresh yourself, and then join us for almuerzo (lunch). Would you also like some coffee?"

"Si, Si," I quickly answered, as I was exhausted.

"I'll get you some delicious Colombian coffee," he said as he excused himself, going back into the living room.

I proceeded to the bathroom and washed my face with cold water, found my electric shaver and shaved. I then hurried back to the dining room and was delightfully presented with a plate full of fruit and the first of many beautiful mugs of Colombian coffee with milk, which I quickly engulfed.

I told Padre Gabriel the reasons for me coming to Colombia and what I intended to accomplish.

We sat down at the kitchen table and Padre Gabriel introduced Maria, a private cook, who would fix most of the meals during the time I stayed with Los Tres Padres. Maria brought everyone at the table a beautifully prepared lunch of chicken and rice, along with more fresh fruit and vegetables.

After an extremely delicious meal, I started discussing with Padre Gabriel his history and his childhood, how and when he was born, in el campo or la finca, countryside or farmland outside of Cali, Colombia. His mother's name was Gabriella Montoya and Padre Gabriel was her second pregnancy. She was quite sick with morning sickness during the pregnancy and went into premature labor after 8 months. While in labor, Padre Gabriel's head would not come out of the birth canal, so Gabriella prayed to Saint Antonio Maria Claret to save the life of her baby son and promised, if Gabriel lived, she would dedicate him to serve God, the church, seminary and priesthood.

His father, Carlos Arturo Mejia, left Gabriella laboring to obtain the services of a local doctor, who happened to be inebriated. The doctor delivered Gabriel with forceps, causing damage to his head and skull at birth (birth trauma to the skull with forceps was a very common occurrence in the 1940's and 50's). Padre Gabriel added, "I believe my birth trauma, with the forceps, caused me emotionally to have much anxiety and fear for the first six years of my life." I thought of how I had learned of these birth traumas causing emotional problems throughout life, long after I had quit delivering babies and started to do trauma release techniques to assist in healing these trapped emotions.

Padre Gabriel went on, "My childhood was wonderful, growing up in a family which loved me, living out in the country with fresh foods, fruits and vegetables, picked right from the plants and trees. We played as children with all the neighboring children and our entire community had a sense of belonging. We went to a small local school, which just taught simple teachings of reading, basic math, and spelling, but my mother was my primary source of education. We would read together, write stories, and learned algebra and geometric math."

Padre Gabriel continued, "My childhood was very happy and my parents were very good to me. Growing up in the farmlands (la finca) of Colombia, up in the mountains near Cali, Colombia, was very healthy. My mother used herbal remedies for the family and children's health, and was always preparing the best of local fruits and vegetables for the children to eat.

"My father, Carlos Arturo Mejia, had a lot of land for growing coffee beans, mangos and papayas with hired help from the community. He was a great businessman, doing negotiations for all kinds of agriculture, especially coffee, taking products from the Highlands to the larger city of Cali, Colombia, and bringing products back for the people. My father took me many times with him and I was able to learn about business, negotiating, trading and taking care of people.

My father would often help the people of our pueblo, sometimes making nothing or even losing money in the process monetarily, but producing much good will, always being compassionate and aware of the people's needs. My father was loved by all and shared his wealth, which was not much because of always giving it away." Padre Gabriel said, "I felt rich even though we didn't have a lot of money. My father took care of everyone he would meet. My mother, however, taught me more about relationships and how to be loving and compassionate.

"My mother, Gabriella, was very intelligent and a great cook and spent a lot of time teaching the children and reading to them from books. Living in the mountains of Colombia, we lived a very rural life and the schools provided a very basic education." Padre Gabriel added, "My mother filled in most of the missing pieces of my education. She was always happy, and this happy demeanor filled my life with happiness, pleasure and a desire for all children to have a full happy life like my own."

Padre Gabriel continued, "I left home at 14 years old and joined the Claretian seminary in Bogotá where I studied to become a Priest. I was just a child, but very determined to serve God for sparing my life, completing the promise of my Mother to God.

"When I was 16 years old, while in the Priesthood Seminary in Bogotá, I had severe gastrointestinal problems for several months and started vomiting up blood. I was diagnosed with a bleeding ulcer and told to change my eating habits by the specialist in Bogotá, to only eat very bland and simple foods, with fresh vegetables and fruits, which I have continued to do all these years. Simple fresh food is what we feed the children and adults in our Hogares Claret. Fresh food is an important therapy to heal and stay strong," Padre Gabriel emphasized.

Padre Gabriel continued, "My older Brother, Carlos, now 74 years old, had meningitis and polio while only a child of six months old, which caused his entire left side of his body to be paralyzed. For many years, our mother worked every day, for hours at a time, helping Carlos to learn how to walk and use his left leg, left arm and hands, and helped us study, read, write, and become useful around the house and yard. The polio slowly started to heal and with layman's physical therapy from our mother, Carlos improved little by little and the left side of his body started healing, so Carlos became a miracle. His body slowly repaired, and Carlos became more active, but only due to the efforts of our mother and the constant prayers of the family." Padre Gabriel got tears in his eyes and continued, "To this day Carlos is totally functional and improved and works as if he has no problems," Padre Gabriel stated.

Continuing about Carlos, "At the age of 15 years old, Carlos had an aptitude for fixing things and was blessed with very excellent ability to build and use electronics. Carlos became very adept and started to work with companies to build and repair electronics in Colombia.

At the age of 20, Carlos left Colombia to work in the United States finding good paying jobs in New Jersey, later working for Toys"R"Us. Carlos has lived in the United States for 54 years, created many toys and electronics and worked on many projects for Toys"R"Us before retiring with a very good pension. He returned to Colombia many times to visit his family; however, due to his love of the United States and a good paying job, he spent most of his time at work in New Jersey," stated Padre Gabriel.

Padre Gabriel finished about his brother, "The love of his mother and her patience, prayers and love, with Carlos, healed the firstborn of our family."

Padre Gabriel, 72 years old, is the second son, whose story is the topic of this book.

"Carmemza, 70 years old, the first daughter, third child, lives in Cali, has three sons with good health and 10 grandchildren, but was separated from her husband recently. They are separate, but she is still good friends with her husband," Gabriel added. "She lives a good life, is in good health, and has not lacked for anything."

"Our Mejia family Adopted Delli, a second girl, when she was very young. She is now 75 years old, lives in Brazil, and is married to Nino Crime. He is the Director of Opera in Brazil, S.A. He is a high professor of music and is recognized even in New York in the United States. They are parents of Nino Crime, Jr., who is also a very famous musician with talent in opera and other productions and is a director of music in the United States and Brazil," continued Padre Gabriel.

"Mercedes, 69 years old, lives in Cali and continued the family company of shirt production started by her mother when times were tough. She did very well continuing her mother's business; the shirt factory is very famous in Colombia. Mercedes developed cancer of the lungs with metastasis of 17 tumors into her brain and other parts of her body. The family prayed for her for three years and she was cured of her cancer. The family and friends prayed and manifested for her to recover, praying 7 AM to 7 PM for three years using healing techniques from the healing codes written by Gregg Braden. She is still alive and doing well," stated Padre Gabriel.

"In 1948, politician Jorge Elie'cer Gaitan Ayala, former Mayor of Bogotá, Education Minister of Colombia (1940) and labor minister of Colombia (1943-1944) became a candidate for President of Colombia of the Liberal Party. Carlos Mejia, my father, helped to manage his efforts to be elected. Jorge was assassinated during his candidacy for President of Colombia by a deranged man. My father, who had been supporting Gaitan's presidential election, became a scapegoat to the people in the surrounding community and this caused him to lose most of his money, including his land and all his businesses," continued Padre Gabriel.

"It was a very heavy time for the Mejia family," remembered Padre Gabriel, "but my parents continued to work hard during those difficult three-four years. My mother, Gabriella, sewed shirts for the people in the community surrounding Cali, Colombia, doing such fine work that in 1951, she started a shirt making company which supported the family during these hard times. Later Mercedes took over the shirt factory in Cali, Colombia, which now has over 200 employees and is still doing well and making money for Mercedes and her family."

Chapter 3 - Padre Gabriel's Injury

Forty-five days prior to my arrival in Medellín, Colombia, Padre Gabriel was hit multiple times in the face and forehead with a large rock, by one of the resident adolescent orphans of the Hogares Claret, which broke seven teeth and seven bones in his face including the zygomatic arches on both sides and breaking some bones in the maxillary sinuses, as well as general damage to his face. It knocked Padre Gabriel unconscious, and he was taken to the local hospital where he was stabilized. During those 45 days prior to my arrival in Colombia, Father Gabriel had undergone several surgeries including reconstructive surgery. A cadaver bone had been placed in his jaw to repair and improve his bite.

By the time I arrived, June 1st, after a month and half of surgeries and recovering, Padre Gabriel had started physical therapy, receiving light and laser treatments and other alternative therapy with the professional doctors there in Medellín.

I had intuited something was going on prior to my leaving to go to Colombia, so I packed several herbs for infection and inflammation into my bag for Colombia. I also brought herbs which provide nutrition for hair, bones, ligaments, joints and damaged tissue. When I met Padre Gabriel Mejia, with my intuitive sight I could see infection in his mouth, maxillary, ethmoid, sphenoid, and frontal sinuses and face, so I asked Padre Gabriel if he would like to take some herbs to help his condition in addition to what he was taking from his practitioners there in Colombia.

Padre Gabriel smiled and said, "Seguro que si," which translated means "For sure yes."

Padre Gabriel immediately began taking the herbs, and I could see improvement every day.

There was also an energy behind Padre Gabriel's third eye. This caused an uneasiness and pain in his head, which was difficult for him to describe. He would say, "There is something wrong here, in the front of my mind, blocking clarity of thinking and spiritual communion." I asked, "Can I do some energy work with the help of the Archangels, St. Germaine and Jesus to help remove the negative energy?" Padre Gabriel again agreed, and we began the process of removing those energies. They had entered into his skull and auric field with the heavy blows from the possessed teenager, causing the uneasiness which Padre Gabriel was experiencing.

I asked the two other Fathers, Padre José and Padre Orlando, to assist me in giving a laying on of hands or a Priesthood blessing to Padre Gabriel, to assist with his healing for his best and highest good. I anointed the Crown Chakra of Father Gabriel's head with a drop of consecrated olive oil from the olive trees in the Garden of Gethsemane, outside the walls of Jerusalem, which I carry in my traveling bag. Then I asked the other two Fathers to place their hands on Padre Gabriel's head, and I proceeded to bless him with the following words in Spanish, "Padre Gabriel Antonio Mejia-Montoya, In the name of the Father, and of the Son and of the Holy Spirit, we place our hands upon your head, to give you a blessing from God. We command the negative entities which have been tormenting you to be removed now! We call forth the Light and Love from God to heal you, now! We Bless you, that you will be filled with the healing power of the ascended Masters, and that you continue forward with the power of God, to continue your work upon the earth with Power, Love and Wisdom. We Bless the bones, ligaments, tendons and flesh of your face and head to heal, and that the pain you are experiencing will be removed. We seal this Blessing upon you, in the name del Padre, del Nino y del Espiritu Santo, Amen." The blessing was finished and a beautiful energy emanated from the other Padres. Padre Gabriel stood up, with a sparkle in his eyes, and turned and hugged each one of us, expressing gratitude and love.

Chapter 4 - Medellín, Colombia and Panama

Antioquia is a mountainous area of Northwestern Colombia, nearest to Panama. The Caribbean Sea lies to the north and Pacific Ocean to the west. Medellín became the provincial government center and capital of the District of Antioquia.

Panama was actually a province of Colombia to the north of Antioquia over 120 years ago, prior to the United States displaying her political and military power, causing the secession of the northernmost province of Colombia. The United States first negotiated with the Government of Colombia to build the Panama Canal, and a treaty was made with the Provincial Diplomats. The National Congress in Bogotá voted against the treaty, refusing to ratify, so President Theodore Roosevelt of the United States flexed the muscles of the United States Naval forces, sending in two destroyer convoys, one to Colón on the Caribbean and one to Panama City, "liberating" Panama and paying the new government for a ten mile wide stretch of land from the Atlantic Ocean to the Pacific Ocean, contracting to build the Panama Canal.

Completed in 1914, the Panama Canal symbolized U.S. technological prowess and economic and military power. Although U.S. control of the canal eventually became an irritant to U.S.-Panamanian relations, at the time it was heralded as a major foreign policy achievement. However, the treatment of Panama as a sovereign nation by the United States would always be an irritant to the Colombian people.

Antioquia is the sixth largest Department of Colombia. It is predominantly mountainous, crossed by the *Cordillera Central* and the *Cordillera Occidental* of the Andes. The Cordillera Central further divides to form the Aburrá valley, in which the capital Medellín is located.

The Cordillera Central forms the plateaus of Santa Rosa de Osos and Rio Negro, where the Medellín International airport is located, called José María Córdova International Airport. It is the second largest airport in Colombia after El Dorado International Airport of Bogotá in terms of infrastructure and passenger service.

Despite 80% of the Department's territory being mountainous, which keeps temperatures in the moderate range, it is located near the equator and has a tropical climate. Antioquia also has lowlands in Bajo Cauca, Magdalena Medio, and eastern Sonsón as well as a coast on the Caribbean Sea, in Urabá. This area is of high strategical importance due to its location on both the Atlantic and Pacific oceans.

The facts about Antioquia and the Medellín International airport are courtesy of *Wikepedia*.

The facts about the Panama Canal are courtesy of the U.S. Office of the Historian.

Chapter 5 - Day 2 in Colombia

Tuesday June 2, 2015

I awoke feeling very refreshed, sleeping well in the cool night air of the high mountains just outside of Medellín, Colombia. I had been awakened with the pitter patter of an early morning rain, which, I discovered would occur each night between 4-5 AM. In the other room I could hear the Catholic Fathers celebrating Mass, then all became quiet as they did their Transcendental Meditation.

Father Gabriel told me the night before that breakfast would be served at 8 AM the next morning in the dining room. I walked out of my room to the living room door and unlocked the fancy Colombian lock mechanism, which took me a minute to figure out. I opened the door carefully, so as not to disturb the three Fathers, and went out to enjoy the sounds of tropical birds and bugs chirping in the crisp, beautiful morning, with the sun peeking over the mountains in the east, bringing light to a beautiful tropical paradise. My iPhone was not working on the network in Colombia, but Facetime with the internet worked perfectly. I called Vicki with Facetime back home in St. George, Utah, letting her know I had arrived in Colombia, that I was safe, and had very nice accommodations. I told her about my first day in Colombia meeting Camilo and Los Tres Padres, or The Three Fathers. She was happy to see my happy face and surroundings with Facetime.

Vicki also related how it had taken a lot of faith to put me on a plane, going on a trip to a country like Colombia, with a reputation of being the murder capital of the world.

I discussed how Providence watched over me at the various airports and how helpful all the people I had met the first day had been, arriving in this wonderful country. I talked about how safe I felt, staying with the Three Fathers and their kindness opening up their home to me.

I could see the reassurance in Vicki's countenance as we spoke to one another. Lost in our conversation for over an hour, I could feel the love and commitment of my sweet wife supporting me on yet another adventure to South America.

On our last trip to Peru in 2013, Vicki had experienced getting parasites, and then an E. coli infection, which had caused an erosive gastritis, leaky gut syndrome, in which macro-molecules of undigested foods were absorbed and released into her bloodstream causing her immune system to attack these foods as foreign invaders.

She quickly lost muscle mass and weight, as her allergies to food increased over the following months. She ended up in bed, with no energy, horrible abdominal pain and body aches. Her family could see her getting sicker and sicker, and urged me to take her to the hospital. I knew they would not be able to help her and would tell her she had gastritis. Despite my intuition, I drove Vicki to the ER and checked her into the local hospital in St. George.

The nurse hooked up an IV as her blood pressure was quite low, knowing we had a long wait ahead of us. After hours of blood testing, x-rays and ultrasound of the abdomen, giving her IV fluids due to her dehydration, the emergency room doctor walked in with only a diagnosis of gastritis and dehydration, and prescribed a medication to calm down her stomach and intestines, then sent us home, only giving us more questions about her condition.

Luckily, we had become friends with an acupuncturist who recommended using a blood test with a company called ALCAT to check for food allergies. The testing results confirmed our worries and showed that Vicki was allergic to all the foods tested, except for seven basic foods. We reduced her foods to these and started to cook bone broth, convalescing her bowel and reducing her pain, which slowly improved. Weeks passed and slowly her allergies to the other foods were reduced using homeopathic remedy vials charged with energy of each particular food, taped to her skin for 24-48 hours.

Vicki, having become so sick after traveling to Peru, decided not to accompany me to Colombia.

With God's help and great friends in alternative medicine, she had improved, but was leery of traveling to foreign lands. That is why I was traveling alone. I could hear the Three Fathers in the kitchen and told Vicki, "I love you. I'll call you tomorrow," and ended the Facetime call.

Chapter 6 - Day 2 in Colombia (Continued)

Tuesday June 2, 2015

I entered the house through the beautiful wooden door and quickly walked into the dining room, not wanting to be late. Padre Gabriel was already seated, sipping on some hot Colombian cocoa. "Buenos dias, Dr. Scott," he announced. Father Orlando and Father Joseph entered the dining area quickly with me.

Maria brought in several bowls of fruit and eggs. I felt right at home. We said a blessing on the food and I began to enjoy my first breakfast in Colombia.

While we were eating, Padre Gabriel asked, "What would Dr. Scott like to do as an itinerary for your time in Medellín?" I told Padre Gabriel, "I want to go everywhere you go, do everything you do, and be with you as much as possible. I'm here to learn about you and your programs. If you need to do other things privately, I could go with you and write as you are in meetings or sessions where I cannot be." Padre Gabriel nodded with satisfaction, "I am glad you are here Dr. Scott, but I need to know, what is your goal?"

I thought and answered, "I'm here to write a book about you and the work you are doing. I'm here to be of service and learn as much as I can in the next two weeks." Father Gabriel smiled and nodded agreeably to this plan, even though it was a little too loose for him. "Let me know if you are getting the knowledge and experience you need. We will take good care of you while you are here." Father Gabriel wasn't used to my just being led by spirit. Father Gabriel's days were always purposeful and well planned, well in advance.

The breakfast was so fresh, fruit picked right off the trees outside and eggs from the hens in the chicken coop out back. When breakfast was completed, we packed up our bags, walked out the door, past the wooden porch, down the rock and cement path, around the archery range, making a sharp left past the shelter for the archery range, and continued upon the path to the lower buildings, to a clean, white, 4-door Volkswagen Golf. Multiple varieties of roses and tropical flowers, beautifully groomed, lined the entire path.

Father Joseph enjoyed doing the driving and Father Gabriel let him. Father Gabriel made calls and received messages on his phone, getting the latest news from the people working for the Hogares Claret, while Father Joseph drove the 30 minutes to downtown Medellín, ending up on Avenida Oriental International, the main road and corridor through the valley. Father Joseph made a left turn to drop Father Orlando off at one of the Hogares Claret in the downtown area, then merged through what seemed to be impassable traffic back onto Avenida Oriental and made a right turn off the main road onto a small one-way street. He pushed a remote control as we entered a long, one-car garage filled with three motorcycles, two blocks off the main road. We had arrived at the main offices of Hogares Claret.

We exited the Volkswagen and entered the building, where Padre Gabriel was greeted by the secretary and several other people, mugs of Colombian coffee in hand, at the front desk. One by one, all the people of the main offices of Hogares Claret were introduced to me by Father Gabriel, and they each shook my hand vigorously. We made our way to Padre Gabriel's office upstairs, and I was introduced to the people in many rooms, on the left, then the right, down a long hall. I met John, with a toothy, protruding smile, who had recently moved to Medellín. He had been in charge of the Boy Scouts of Colombia in

Bogotá, and now had been hired to work at the Hogares Claret and all the homes for the children in the mountainous regions nearby.

Padre Gabriel retrieved several things from his office for a meeting in Santa Elena, up in the mountains of Medellín. Camilo Estrella arrived, shaking my hand and stating in English, "Dr. Scott, so good to see you again." I returned the greeting with, "It's my pleasure," in Spanish. Camilo asked, "How did you learn such formal Spanish?" I explained, "I served a service mission for the Church of Jesus Christ of Latter-Day Saints in south Florida and Puerto Rico for two years when I was a young man like you." Camilo laughed, "You'll fit in perfectly. Your Spanish is like the formality of the Clergy, but without the regional accent added."

I followed Camilo and John with Padre Gabriel out of the front entrance, to a white 16-passenger van, where we were joined by two of the women workers from the central office. We traveled about 15 miles through the city to the other side of the valley, leaving the city behind us. We continued up into the cool fresh air of the Andes mountains to a beautiful forest of tall pine trees. The road became less occupied with cars, motorcycles and trucks.

Soon, around 9:45 AM, we found ourselves high in the mountains surrounding Medellín, where the air was clean, cool, and crisp. As we passed by several horse pastures and corrals, Padre Gabriel explained how equine therapy was being introduced and used in Santa Elena as an emotional release technique for sexual abuse and for drug rehabilitation.

We then drove past a large set of new buildings being constructed, and Padre Gabriel explained, "This is a new K-12 school which is being built jointly for the local population's use in Santa Elena, as well as for the students of the foundation and children of local Government employees."

We entered another area of new construction surrounding a large white five-story building of neo-modern architecture. We pulled the van around a large circular gravel driveway where there was spacious parking in front of the large white building. I asked, "What is this building?" and was answered, by Father Gabriel, "This is our residence for adult men, 18 years and older in the program of Hogares Claret. We have art, jewelry, woodworking, auto mechanical and small machine repair, leather working, and other programs for the men. We provide the resources which will help the men reintegrate back into the workforce with excellent training from volunteers and previous graduates."

We pulled up to the beautiful building which had a large slope in the back and a huge glass-covered arborarium. I was told by Father Gabriel, "The building was purchased from the South American Society of Transcendental Meditation, and it had been previously been owned by followers of Maharishi Mahesh Yogananda.

About a dozen men surrounded the van as we parked in front of the building on the gravel road. Smiles were on all their faces and they happily greeted us, especially happy to see Father Gabriel. "Buenos dias, Buenos dias," they were practically shouting as they welcomed us to the facility.

Father Gabriel introduced me, "This is Dr. Scott from the United States of America. He has come to learn about Hogares Claret in Santa Elena. Please give him your best attention while he is here."

Having me there as their guest, they wanted me to come see what they were doing. Instead of going to the main entrance, we walked to the right side of the building and entered through a large white metal door to an adjacent area where residents were living. They happily showed me their rooms and living areas and the project areas where they were doing woodworking and leather working. They also had an area where they proudly were making jewelry and metal works, a large modern auto shop and small engine repair shop. The men also showed me a library where a circle of about 50 men were holding a group therapy meeting.

When the leader saw us enter, he quickly stopped speaking, got out of his chair and walked over to where we were. You could feel the love in his voice, "Father Gabriel, thank you so much for your visit today. Please join us." Padre Gabriel introduced me as Dr. Scott as we walked to the far end of the room where the men were gathered. We sat down and listened to the discussion for about 15 minutes. Then, the leader of the discussion asked Father Gabriel to address the group. Father Gabriel gave a wonderful discourse about the progress of the foundation and the success of the rehabilitation and integration of the children and adults. He expressed his love for the men and women of the program and their hard work. He talked about how love was changing the world and all the people in it.

Father Gabriel told the men that I was his personal guest and that I was there to observe the progress of the foundation so they should openly discuss with me their rehabilitation progress and where they had come from and how successful the programs of the foundation of Hogares Claret had been for them. He asked several volunteers of the residents to tell their story.

One young man stood and asked to go first. He introduced himself and stated that the foundation had saved his life. He was living on the street, prostituting for money, using alcohol and drugs, and stealing from anyone he could take advantage of. He found himself in the gutter many times, barely alive. He decided, as he was lying dirty and soaking wet with rain coming down upon him, that there had to be something better. For the first time in his life, he asked God for help. He heard a voice say, "Hogares Claret." He had heard about the

Hogares Claret from one of the other homeless people. He decided in that instant, exhausted, wet and cold in the muddy street, he would seek out and join Hogares Claret without hesitation, to better his life. He expressed his gratitude to Father Gabriel, that because he had become so happy with the changes in his life by becoming part of the program, he had stayed on working at Hogares Claret to help others in the organization, and had remained for six years. He was now a leader in the organization, living with the other men, helping and becoming an instructor to improve all their lives. Many similar stories came from the mouths of the men in room.

Another one of the many men in the library asked to be heard. "I was living in the street, using drugs and alcohol to drown my pain. I had been told about Father Gabriel and the foundation. My only friend was just like me, dying from drugs and alcohol, lying and stealing when we could. We looked at each other, shivering, one cold and rainy night. We decided to see about the Hogares Claret. We were tired of dying a little bit more each day in the streets. We joined the program. Now we are rehabilitated and clean, we both have learned vocations, earn money and feel loved and happy, thanks to the Hogares Claret and Father Gabriel."

Another young man stood up and started sobbing, barely able to speak. He had told another street person that he was ready to end his life and commit suicide. As he was about to drink old gasoline, an Angelic voice stopped him and told him instead, "Find Father Gabriel, and join with his Hogares Claret program." This gave him hope. He found Hogares Claret and Father Gabriel, and has been in the foundation ever since with happiness and peace in his soul and a purpose for living.

Yet another young man stood up telling a similar story. He found himself in the gutter many times barely alive, due to drug overdoses and beatings. A young boy appeared to him, saying, "We both should join ourselves to the Hogares Claret foundation to better our lives."

He recognized this young boy and agreed with him, "Nobody should live like this, not knowing where our next meal will come from or where we will sleep that night." That day, both of them, with heavenly intervention, found the foundation and had been there ever since. He expressed his gratitude for that eventful day.

Several other men told their stories, which were similar. Many of them had started out in the streets as young children, abandoned and alone. Many were doing whatever it took to get food, money and shelter to stay alive. Each man cried with gratitude as he told his story. Father Gabriel gazed at each of them with compassion and love.

Father Gabriel then stood and addressed the group. He spoke with authority and yet a humbleness of soul and spirit, "I am so grateful for your words of gratitude and thankfulness. The Lord Jesus is looking upon us today with a smile. He sends his love and I give my love to you all for speaking about the truth and enlightening all of us with your stories. Please listen carefully to Dr. Scott, who has traveled far from the United States of America to join us today and learn about the Hogares Claret. He was sent to us to learn and write a book. I would like him to speak to us now."

Father Gabriel motioned to me with his hand, permitting me a chance to speak. As I stood up, speaking in my limited Spanish, I thanked them for their love and acceptance to have me in their presence, and I expressed my gratitude for their beautiful stories. I told them, "Your lives matter, you are important. Your past of suffering, barely living each day and night in the streets, where you have come from, has taught you many important lessons." I continued and told them, "You are the future of the world. The hardships and trials which you have experienced, have taught you how to be the leaders of tomorrow.

Because of the compassion you have experienced through the Hogares Claret, you will be able to help others with compassion in similar situations. Experience is the hardest teacher, but sometimes the most necessary teacher."

I continued, "I grew up in a neighborhood in Utah, in the United States of America, where everyone believes we are privileged. Yes we do have opportunity, but after my dad and mom were divorced I lived in abject poverty. All the clothes and shoes I wore were handed down to me from my older brother and uncle. I experienced many problems, but luckily I didn't have to live in the streets. I was made fun of by the other kids in the school I attended, but at least I was able to go to school and learn, despite my having attention deficit/hyperactivity disorder."

I got a little emotional, but continued, "Luckily when I was 10 years old, my mother remarried a construction engineer. We started eating better food, fruits and vegetables, living a better lifestyle, and I actually felt I had a place in the community and society. With the better nutrition, my hyperactivity went away and my grades and social life improved. Growing up with a mother at home and a father who took care of us was a new experience for me, a better experience and life. My mother and stepfather were well educated and helped me see the importance of educating myself and going to college.

"I decided to go on a service mission for the Mormon church which is the predominant church in Utah. The service I performed for people and the lessons I learned from the service gave me a desire to continue my education. During the mid part of my mission in Puerto Rico, I was hit by a car and woke up with a sheet over my head in the hospital in San Juan, Puerto Rico. I had been declared dead and was on my way down to the morgue in the basement of the hospital. I threw the sheet from my head and sat up, which started the nurses screaming, "Estaba muerta, estaba muerta." I told them, "I'm not dead, I am very much alive." And to this they started screaming for the doctor. My previous x-rays showed multiple broken bones and tissue damage. The doctor who had declared me dead now wanted to do more x-rays, which he did. The new x-rays showed all of my bones were totally normal, although there was some swelling of the tissues and organs.

"When I came back alive from the accident, I knew I was to become a medical doctor helping all of those around me. That same voice which told me to become a medical doctor told me to come to South America, to Medellín, Colombia, to get to know Father Gabriel Mejia and write a book about the miracles being done here in your country. Thank you for your time and stories."

When I was done talking they all laughed and smiled with approval. Father Gabriel and I stood, and I followed Father Gabriel, who started slowly around the circle of men, hugging each person, introducing me to each one of them and greeting each of the men with handshakes and hugs. Father Gabriel spoke to each man by name and told each one the love he felt for them.

After we had completed the entire circle of men, Father Gabriel announced to me, "I have a meeting I need to attend," so he left me in the care of Camilo, who enthusiastically showed me around rest of the facility.

Chapter 7 - Panchakarma

Camilo is in charge of the Institute of Panchakarma at the Santa Elena Hogares Claret, which is a cleansing and rejuvenating program of body-mind consciousness. It is known for its beneficial effect on overall health and wellness, and for its self-healing, stress-releasing and detoxing qualities.

Camilo told me he had started his life of living on the street at a very early age, like many other Colombian boys, but the eventful day he signed up as a resident of the Hogares Claret when he was 13 years old changed the direction of his life forever.

Camilo is very intelligent, and with all the changes that had occurred in his life with Hogares Claret, he desired to stay, becoming a leader with the foundation, teaching others and helping them with their problems. Because of his intellect and leadership abilities, he applied for and received a four-year scholarship to attend Maharishi University of Management in the United States of America from the David Lynch Foundation. Camilo graduated with a Secondary School Certificate from his studies in Medellín, said his goodbyes to his many friends in Hogares Claret, and left, traveling to Fairfield, Iowa, in the United States with the blessing of Father Gabriel.

Camilo stated, "Not being proficient in English and attending Maharishi University of Management for four years on scholarship put a lot of pressure on me to succeed. Until I mastered the English language, I needed much tutoring and help in understanding the basic courses. Ayruvedic Medicine became my focus, but was a whole different language and study in itself. The multi-cultural environment of Maharishi University of Management brought students with diversity and knowledge from all over the world. All the students helped each other, not only with English, but it felt like a 'World University,' as we learned about the diversity of cultures and the various countries."

Camilo continued, "Ayurveda is the world's most ancient system of preventive health care. Developed in India over 6,000 years ago. Ayurveda (which translates as 'knowledge of life') is a natural approach for creating balance and strengthening the body's healing abilities. I focused my energies studying Ayurvedic Medicine, specializing in Panchakarma, learning Panchakarma at the 'Raj,' a beautiful recreation and education center in Fairfield, Iowa. After graduating, I desired to return to the foundation in Colombia using the knowledge and techniques I had learned in Fairfield to help cleanse and detoxify the residents here in Santa Elena.

"Padre Gabriel agreed and gave me the assignment to start the program with the foundation." Camilo motioned for me to walk with him. We left his office and walked down a beautiful walkway on the second floor, which was a balcony among many balconies below a huge, beautifully lighted arborarium. Stopping at each room, Camilo described for me all of the various treatment rooms which they had created and built for doing Panchakarma treatments on visitors and residents. The program at Santa Elena was brand new, just getting started with training from Camilo.

Camilo said as we walked, "We do an Ayurvedic massage called Abhyanga, which is a choreographed massage by one or two well-trained therapists, promoting relaxation, energy flow and purifying of the mind and body. An evaluation is done with the individual by a questionnaire and personal evaluation by the therapist to determine the imbalances of the doshas (energies) in the individual. Personalized essential oils promoting the individual's doshas are used during the massage."

Camilo continued, "Each of us is made up of a combination of the three types of doshas: Vatha, Pitta and Kapha. The doshas as a group are comprised of these five universal elements:

1. Spirit (ether)
2. Air
3. Earth
4. Fire
5. Water

Vatha is a combination of air and spirit.

Pitta is mostly fire with some water.

Kapha is mostly water with some earth."

Camilo continued, "Overall well-being and thriving energy depends on maintaining your health and spirit, in order to keep your doshas balanced. Any imbalance among the three doshas causes a state of unhealthiness, or dis-ease. Factors that can bring about balance of the three doshas include diet, exercise, good digestion, and elimination of toxins.

"Each room is designed differently and assigned for one of five separate treatments and several assistants are doing sessions on each other to perfect the treatments," Camilo explained as he guided me around to each room. I came to find out, in the first room we stopped, that one of the assistants was Camilo's newlywed wife of three months. I learned what treatments were administered in each room.

Shirodhara is performed in the first room, which works specifically on balancing and stabilizing the activity of the mind. Warm dosha-specific oils and herbs are poured over the Ajna Chakra or third eye, taking the patient on a journey deep into oneness and compassion. This treatment is good for mental and emotional balance. It also helps with disorders of the nervous system.

Swedana is a relaxing steam treatment with aromatic medicinal herbs, including lavender, eucalyptus, chamomile, rosemary, lemongrass and bay leaf, which helps to clear energy channels, relax the muscles and clear blocked emotions and toxins. It can follow a massage or be followed with a therapeutic massage.

Marma Point Massage is in the next room, which is a massage that balances 108 energy points in order to balance the various doshas. It works on correcting specific conditions using pranic energy and specific oils to dampen energy points, stimulate energy points or simply even out the energy of the 108 energy points. This treatment is good for mental and emotional balance, nervous system disorders, pain, paralysis and cancer.

Abhyanga Massage is a one- or two-person warm massage involving full body therapeutic massage with essential oils, designed to nourish the tissues, provide deep relaxation to the muscles and calmness to the nerves and mind. Each person is unique and the oils used are different for each individual's needs. The treatment is especially good for muscle tension, chronic fatigue syndrome, fibromyalgia, multiple sclerosis, depression, Parkinson's disease, detoxification and stress reduction.

Nasya treatment begins with a facial massage and heat therapies to the face and forehead, followed with nasal administration of herbal oils and tinctures to purify and clean the sinuses. It helps with allergies, sinusitis, tinnitus, snoring, sleep apnea, headaches, brain fog and mental focus.

Garshana is an exfoliating two-person massage with silk or wool gloves, which rids the skin of dead cells and stimulates lymphatic circulation and removes stagnation. It creates soft, lustrous skin and sub-dermal circulation, removing toxins from the body.

Dough Basti uses a raised circle of dough with specific medicated herbal oils in the center to treat specific conditions and areas of the body:

Eye pain: Netra Basti for glaucoma, cataracts, pink eye, allergies and other eye conditions

Thyroid conditions: Vishuddha Basti for conditions of the thyroid and throat chakra

Thoracic and Lumbar pain: Kati Basti for conditions of the mid and lower back

Heart strength: Uro Basti which strengthens the physical (triple warmer) and emotional heart centers as well as the immune center of the thymus

Hormone balance: Sacral chakra Basti for reproductive system imbalance, reprogramming the hormones, energetic and emotional imbalance in the sexual organs

Anuvasana Basti uses a medicated essential oil enema for detoxification, tonifying and cleansing the colon and root chakra coccyx dual plexus of nerves, removing excess vata from the body.

Niruha Basti uses a medicated herbal tea decoction enema for removal of ama (toxins) from the colon and body

Pinda Swedana uses a bolus of rice and nourishing herbal infusions to treat neuromuscular and skeletal disorders

After Camilo described each room and its function in detoxing the body, we retreated back to Camilo's office where he went on to discuss the doshas. Camilo did the following outline from memory, writing it down for me on a white board:

Body Structures and Characteristics of the 3 Doshas

Dosha Type	Body Structure	Characteristics
Vata	Slender frame	Often constipated
	Lightweight bone structure	Little perspiration
	Dry, rough or dark skin	Sparse urine (although frequent)
	Brown / black hair coloring	Poor long-term memory
	Large, crooked or protruding teeth and gums	Good short-term memory
	Small thin lips and mouth	Anxiety, nervousness, depression
	Dull, dark eyes	High sex drive (or none at all)
		Love of travel
		Dislike of cold weather
		Slight to variable appetite

Dosha Type	Body Structure	Characteristics
Pitta	Medium height and build	Sharp / Clear voice
	Fair to reddish complexion and hair coloring	Light sleeper
	Small yellowish teeth, soft gums	Intelligent
	Green / Grayish Eyes	Clear memory
	Average size mouth	Jealous
		Ambitious
		Sexually passionate
		Dislikes hot weather
		Loves luxury
		Loose stools / diarrhea
		Strong appetite
		Thirsty

Dosha Type	Body Structure	Characteristics
Kapha	Large frame	Speaks in slow monotone
	Tends to be overweight	Requires deep sleep
	Thick and pale-colored oily skin	Steady appetite
	Strong white teeth	Heavy sweating
	Blue eyes	Large soft stools
	Full lips / Large mouth	Business oriented
		Good memory
		Passive
		Dislikes cold and damp
		Loves good food
		Enjoys familiar surroundings

Camilo then related all the benefits he had received through the Hogares Claret Foundation. I could feel Camilo's enthusiasm and love for the program and could see how his emotions were perfected in the thoughts of helping others. "I'm so glad that you are here," said Camilo. "Santa Elena is to be internationally renowned for the healing of guests and donors of Father Gabriel's programs which need to be known and utilized."

Chapter 8 - Leaving Santa Elena

Father Gabriel returned from his meetings with the leaders of Santa Elena, telling me it was time to go back down the mountain. As we approached the van, many of the residents gathered around saluting us and showing their love for Father Gabriel.

They kissed the cheek of Father Gabriel for over 15 minutes, one by one, bidding him "Goodbye" and hugging each other and all the other people in the van. Many office staff gathered on the porch, telling Father of their love and hugging him. More workers saluted Father Gabriel and me with goodbyes. "Please come back, and bring your wife," they all stated to me.

As the van circled around the driveway, away from this beautiful white building, I could tell love ruled in the hearts of all those present. The love was palpable and real!

On the drive off the mountain, I asked Father Gabriel, "What is another major philosophy behind your success with Hogares Claret?"

Father Gabriel answered, "Meeting Maharishi Mahesh Yogananda in 1975 at the age of 32 years old, I became interested in the teachings and philosophies of Maharishi, attending his lectures and teachings here at the Meditation Center in Santa Elena. I wrote down many beautiful thoughts and teachings, and I have a book filled with the thoughts and poems of the earlier teachings of Maharishi, which I will show to you."

Father Gabriel continued, "I was taught Transcendental Meditation by Depok Chopra, with the blessing of Maharishi, who also taught me many beautiful philosophies for helping people. I also studied many psychology theories, including Maslow's hierarchy of human needs. This includes providing the basic physiological needs of food, water, warmth and shelter, as well as the basic needs of personal security, financial security, health and well-being, and safety against accidents/illness and their adverse impacts on life.

"We provide these basic needs with the Hogares Claret and provide the next higher category of physiological and psychological needs, being loved and the feeling of belonging. At this next level the basic needs of friendship, intimacy, and family come into being. This is the most important level that Hogares Claret incorporates in the rehabilitation of the children. The child only thrives and evolves when they know they are loved unconditionally. I send them *Bombas de Amor*, or Love Bombs.

"Maslow's next hierarchy of needs up the scale is self-esteem and self-respect, or the physical and psychological human desire to be accepted and valued by self and others. Low self-esteem, or an inferiority complex, may result from imbalances during this level of Maslow's hierarchy. These need to be corrected if the child or young adult is to progress and become self-sufficient. An essential in our human evolution is love and acceptance, built upon by teaching and incorporating of physical and social purpose. When the child feels accepted and loved, miracles happen.

"The next higher part of Maslow's hierarchy is self-actualization, which is also a major teaching of the logotherapy of Viktor Frankl, who I met in Vienna, Austria in 1987. Viktor Frankel believed that to understand and incorporate this level of need into the psychology and physiology, the person must not only achieve mastery of the lower hierarchy, but also be aware of, and assist with, the needs of other human beings. I feel Transcendental Meditation is a very important aspect of self-actualization, and incorporated meditation is an important part of self-esteem, self-awareness and self-actualization.

"The highest form of Maslow's hierarchy is self-transcendence, which includes Transcendental Meditation and service to others.

"Saving the Disposable Ones is a documentary made in 2010 about the children Colombia referred to as the 'disposable ones'. These children were abandoned in the streets of most of the larger cities of Colombia, thousands of children, enduring terrible physical and sexual abuse, enslavement, drug abuse and addiction. The movie describes how the foundation brings them in off the streets to the Hogares Claret, taking them through the steps to heal emotionally, physically and spiritually, and to become contributing human beings. Service is an expression of Unconditional Love."

Chapter 9 - Changing the Daily Business in Colombia

According USHistory.org, "During the campaign of 1980, Ronald Reagan announced a recipe to fix the nation's economic mess. He claimed an undue tax burden, excessive government regulation, and massive social spending programs hampered growth of the American economy. Reagan proposed a phased 30% tax cut for the first three years of his Presidency. The bulk of the cut would be concentrated at the upper income levels. The economic theory behind the wisdom of such a plan was called *supply-side* or *trickle-down* economics. The media called it *Reaganomics*."

Reagan was elected President and Congress sided with the economic mandate in November, 1980. The article from USHistory.org continues, "Tax relief for the rich would enable them to spend and invest more. This new spending would stimulate the economy and create new jobs. Reagan believed that a tax cut of this nature would ultimately generate even more revenue for the federal government. The Congress was not as sure as Reagan, but they did approve a 25% cut during Reagan's first term.

"The results of this plan were mixed. Initially, the Federal Reserve Board believed the tax cut would re-ignite inflation and raise interest rates, which it did. This sparked a deep recession in 1981 and 1982. The high interest rates (18-26%) caused the value of the dollar to rise on the international exchange market, making American goods more expensive abroad. As a result, exports decreased while imports increased. Eventually, the economy stabilized in 1983, and the remaining years of Reagan's administration showed national growth," but a continued double digit prime interest rate climbed till 1986, then slowly started to decrease.

"The defense industry boomed as well. Reagan insisted that the United States was open to a 'window of vulnerability' to the Soviet Union regarding nuclear defense. Massive government contracts were awarded to defense firms to upgrade the nation's military. Reagan even proposed a space-based missile defense system called the Strategic Defense Initiative. Scientists were dubious about the feasibility of a laser-guided system that could shoot down enemy missiles. Critics labeled the plan Star Wars."

The website coldwar.org states, "The Strategic Defense Initiative (SDI), or Star Wars, was a program first initiated on March 23, 1983 under President Ronald Reagan. The intent of this program was to develop a sophisticated Laser-guided, anti-ballistic missile system in order to prevent missile attacks from other countries, specifically the Soviet Union. With the tension of the Cold War looming overhead, the Strategic Defense Initiative was the United States' response to possible nuclear attacks from afar. Although the program seemed to have no negative consequences, there were concerns brought up about the program 'contravening' the anti-ballistic missile (ABM) of the Strategic Arms Limitation Talks years before. For this reason, in conjunction with budgetary constraints, the Strategic Defense Initiative was ultimately set aside. By the end of SDI, the primary focus of the weapons design group was land-based kinetic energy weapons."

These weapons were essentially guided missile projectiles. Because Congress voted against spending the billions of dollars for these or any other missile defense system, President Reagan decided to set the Central Intelligence Agency on several Top Secret, "Black Ops" rogue missions, without oversight of Congress, to produce money within secret programs overseeing drug trafficking and money laundering operations, to the United States, Europe and other rich countries, to make billions of dollars, and to do covert operations to destroy Communism and the Soviet bloc.

With this initiative, and blessing of the President of the United States, the CIA initiated several deep "Black Ops" operations, classified beyond Top Secret, hiring Central and South American businessmen such as Pablo Escobar in Colombia to bring coca leaves into Colombia (Colombia never had drug Cartels prior to 1982) for processing and distribution of finished cocaine alkaloid to the United States and Europe.

The billions of dollars created with this "drug trade" went into super-secret operations of not only Star Wars technology, missiles and kinetic weapons, but also other secret space programs and weapons development. This information is covered in many recently published books such as *Insiders Reveal Secret Space Programs & Extraterrestrial Alliances*, by Michael E. Salla, Ph.D., and *The Secret History of Extraterrestrials*, by Len Kasten. Both of these books cover multiple topics concerning extraterrestrials and discloses the truth about several alien spacecraft crashing near Roswell, New Mexico in July 1947 and the use of reverse engineering of the alien technologies to create the expensive space programs and secret weapons programs. Space and secret weapons programs that were financed secretly with the heartache, money, and enslavement of millions of human beings to drug use, addiction and war crimes with this abominable use of Government agencies.

The secret agencies' activities over almost 70 years became invisible, even within the CIA and other military agencies, yielding clearance levels beyond Top Secret, which were beyond congressional oversight, beyond the judicial and executive branches *need to know*.

This is how cocaine production and distribution became a problem in Colombia and most of South and Central America. And for that matter, the rest of the world. The bankers became major targets and consumers, because "that is where the money is."

Chapter 10 - Father Gabriel's Evolution

Timeline of Father Gabriel's studies of self-actualization and purpose of opening Hogares Claret:

1982: February–July, studied in Italy, under project Humana of Castel Gandolfo's organization Huomo. Attended the presentation of Viktor Frankl in Vienna, Austria where Logotherapy was first presented.

1983: Attended Logotherapy convention of Viktor Frankl, M.D., Ph.D., author of *Man's Search for Meaning*. After this meeting, Father Gabriel thought there should be a foundation started to assist the disposable ones, so he opened the first treatment center in 1983 in Colombia. Under the direction of the Claretian Order, he opened the first Hogares Claret in Medellín Colombia, and within two weeks, there were over 50 people (mostly young adults) enrolled.

1984: August, Father Gabriel opened the first Hogares Claret in Brazil, and within one month had 60 adults enrolled in Buenos Aires, Brazil.

1984: December, opened the second Hogares Claret in Medellín, close to where the Allegra Hogares Claret is today in Estrella, a pueblo of Medellín.

1986: Lancaster, MA, Father Gabriel attended a convention of psychological rehabilitation with Viktor Frankl lecturing, incorporating many new therapies.

1987: Spent time learning alternative medicine and other therapies of transformation with Depok Chopra.

1988: November, Father Gabriel received permission from the Catholic Church to learn Transcendental Meditation from Deepak Chopra.

1989: First visit to Fairfield, Iowa, lecturing with the request of Maharishi speaking for the first time in America at Maharishi University of Management. Father Gabriel learned about Panchakarma in Fairfield, Iowa, at the Raj Resort.

1989: Opened another Hogares Claret, in Envigado, Colombia, Pueblo Grande, the first Hogares Claret for women (Pablo Escobar was from Envigado).

1992-93: Father Gabriel visited and spoke with Pablo Escobar in jail in Envigado to listen and talk with him as a Catholic Priest. When the police would ask for information, Padre Gabriel would just say he was there as a Priest and couldn't talk about the confessions and conversation.

1994: Father Gabriel states, "Prayer takes the soul to God, Meditation brings God into our hearts."

2001: Alan de Villeas de San Pierre Jette, a Count from Belgium, an expert with a new nano technology, including nanobots and artificial intelligence, became good friends with Father Gabriel. After being taught Transcendental Meditation, he decided the technology was too dangerous for the future of humanity. Alan was very influential with Father Gabriel, helping the foundation with funding and resources.

Chapter 11 - The Disposable Ones

The movie, *Saving The Disposable Ones*, released in 2010 and directed by Stewart Tanner, is a compelling documentary film that takes you to the heartbreaking streets of major cities of Colombia, South America, where several extraordinary Claretian Priests, led by Father Gabriel Mejia, are transforming the lives of thousands of children by providing food, shelter, water, education, love and Transcendental Meditation. The street children in Colombia are called "the disposable ones" as they are unloved, unwanted, and endure abuse on many levels.

Father Gabriel has learned through his work with the street children that the desire to move away from their life on the streets must come from within the children themselves. Over time, an extraordinary transformation in the lives of the children takes place. They are freed from the torments they endured living on the streets, recover from their drug and other addictions and begin to gain an education and a resolution of the effects of physical abuse and psychological damage.

Even young adults enter into the programs because they desire to better their lives, which for many years have been affected by the cartels and drug wars.

FATHER GABRIEL'S BELIEF SYSTEM:

Describe your Faith in God?

"God is in everything and in every human. We just have to find the Love within us. Then we find our Faith."

Who and what is God?

"The supreme force which moves the world. God is Love and provides everything we need in our lives. All religions teach of God. All religions are the same. All are true because they all take us to God. The day that the religions come together will bring peace to the earth."

What do you want to leave humanity?

"Bombas de Amor (Bombs of Love)."

What are your desires for the future?

"The future is what we are creating now, and that reveals our future to the universe, creating it for us."

Where do you want to go when this life is over?

"I believe firmly that life doesn't end. Life transforms us and brings us back to God. There, we will be in face-to-face conversation with God about our lives. The fear of death is an error, death doesn't exist. We'd better prepare ourselves for this moment where we contact God and find that we have existed forever and ever.

"Our attachments take us further away from our spirit to meet God. Service to others brings us closer to God. Attachment to objects or things or fear robs us of happiness, takes from us our happiness. The purpose of God is that we be happy!"

Where do you see yourself 10 years from now?

"I want to be where I am at now. I am happy as I am fighting for the people and children I love."

While staying with Father Gabriel, I met two other very dedicated Fathers, Father Orlando Hoyos, who has totally gray/white hair and a cheerful/happy disposition, and Father José Fernando Tobon, who has mixed black and gray hair and is a little more serious, speaking excellent English. Both are in their 70's, and both are cheerful Claretian priests who assist Father Gabriel in the day-to-day work of Hogares Claret. Father José Fernando Tobon was our driver almost every morning. When I wasn't quite getting what Father Gabriel was saying in Spanish, Father José would translate.

Chapter 12 - Day 3 in Colombia

June 3, 2015

Little taps of music on the roof caused me to awaken from the drops of rain around 4 AM in Medellín. The tapping increased and I began to hear little waterfalls hitting the ground from the roof. I had expected more rain being in Colombia, but this was the first heavy rain and I was very soothed by the sounds.

I decided to meditate and go back to sleep. At 6:15 AM, I could hear movement and the reciting of the Celebration of the Mass with the Fathers in the next room, and decided to get up and get my day started.

I called Vicki on Facetime, told her all about my previous day, and before I knew it, Father Gabriel peeked in the door, saying, "Dr. Scott, breakfast is served." I quickly said my goodbyes to Vicki and hurried into the dining room.

Again, Maria had outdone herself with poached eggs, toast, fruit, and Colombian coffee. The Three Fathers, as I called them, greeted me with "Buenos dias, como esta Dr. Scott hoy dia." "Muy bien." I countered, as I sat down to another wonderful Colombian meal.

We left the house at 9 AM to go to another one of the houses of Hogares Claret, after a perfect breakfast made with love by Maria, enjoyed with The Three Fathers. They continued the conversation about the Hogares and the children as we drove, discussing different situations and ways to solve the various problems.

All three of these beautiful men had worked with people their entire lives, and among them, had lifetimes of experiences.

Someone in the street handed us a local paper with political headlines. Father Gabriel handed money out the window, refusing the change. There was no fear or worry about robbery and all the street people were most gracious.

Traffic was moving slowly. We traveled down Avenida Oriental though the center of Medellín. We made a right turn, traveling down a busy one-way side street and pulled off left to a garage door. Padre José opened the door with a remote garage opener and we parked.

This Hogares Claret was purchased in 1983, and is beautiful construction of an earlier period of Medellín. A prominent medical doctor owned the building and property surrounding it. Now, high-rise apartments surround the building on three sides.

We were greeted by the workers with "Buenos dias." Hugs and handshakes were freely given.

"Thirty years ago," Father Gabriel explained, "drug use in the young people was unheard of in Colombia. Families worked together in harmony. Colombia was a very happy place to live and work, to raise a family. Now, much is needed to change Colombia and its people back to being happy and healthy."

Three children with smiles on their faces were busy cleaning a large fish tank at the bottom of the stairs. Each of them stopped what they were doing, greeting me with, "Buenos dias." Each of them was so happy and you could see their tranquility.

Many women and men were busy working in the various offices of the Hogares Claret offices. They each greeted us as we passed by.

Meetings of the employees were being held, with the typical air of a large business, of running a large organization.

We ascended the stairs, made a left, walked down a wide hallway, greeting people as we went, and unlocked the door at the end of the hall on the left. Padre Gabriel escorted me into a beautiful office which used to be the master suite of the medical doctor and his wife who owned the house many years ago. It had a view and stairs leading down to a small swimming pool with a patio for eating. The city had grown up with skyscrapers to the right and behind the Hogares Claret.

Father Gabriel asked me to sit and poured essential oils into a diffuser. "We use essential oils in all the Hogares Claret. The oils light up the olfactory sensory lobe of the brain stimulating safety, comfort and contentment, giving these sensations to all smelling the oils, allowing them to move to higher levels of consciousness. We also use floral essences to help with the atmosphere and attitude of the Hogares Claret," he added.

Father Gabriel pulled out his iPad and appointment book and asked permission to get some important negotiations accomplished. "While I work, if you need anything, please ask. Would you like some coffee?" asked Father Gabriel. I answered, "Yes please," and he made both of us a rich cup of Colombian coffee.

I sat down on a couch next to a wooden doorway leading out to twenty molded concrete steps, winding down to a 16 x 25 ft. swimming pool. Enjoying my space on the couch, I pulled out my iPad mini to start writing.

As I was writing, several employees visited Father Gabriel's office with minor issues and problems, which Father Gabriel addressed with a happy, but very businesslike demeanor. He then placed several calls and attended to the day-to-day business needs of Hogares Claret.

The Three Fathers, Gabriel, José and Orlando, are all part of the leadership of Hogares Claret. They are keenly aware of all the people in their surroundings, very kind and complimentary. I am treated with perfect respect and introduced and welcomed by everyone.

We spent the entire morning in the beautiful central offices. I was occupied with writing and observing the well-oiled machine of

Hogares Claret.

Father Gabriel asked, "May I remove myself as I have a meeting with my employees, which was planned prior to your arrival?" I followed with, "Of course," as he departed down the hallway to a conference room at the far end.

Chapter 13 - Brief History of 1980-90's Medellín

Medellín is a cosmopolitan city of 2.5 million people, 4.7 million in the metropolitan area.

Father Gabriel stated, "Colombia didn't have cocaine or a 'drug problem' in the country prior to thirty years ago. However, this changed in the early-to-mid 1980's, mainly due to decisions made by the Central Intelligence Agency of the United States government to fund clandestine operations to overthrow communism and other 'United States unfriendly' regimes. This led to the trafficking of drugs from South and Central America into the United States. The drugs were sold to middle and higher income people, enslaving them to cocaine and other addictive substances, generating billions of dollars from the efforts of the U.S. government, and others. The Governor of Arkansas at the time, Bill Clinton, was paid and promised money and power by allowing large shipments into the United States through the local airports and airbases. This allowed for easy access to the products of these clandestine operations, beyond the efforts of other agencies such as the Drug Enforcement Agency (DEA), whose job is to protect us from the illicit drug trade.

Father Gabriel continued, "The operations of drug trafficking caused an environment of war and abuse in Colombia and other South American countries, the United States of America, Canada, and European countries, which monetarily, physically, emotionally and spiritually resulted in corruption of the people, enslavement of their souls, and death to their spirits.

"Due to this large operation of cocaine production, trade and distribution, money in the billions of dollars started the drug wars. This infiltrated the minds of a peaceful and simple society with greed and all the sins associated with it, leading to corruption of the souls of the people involved. Colombia and her people, and those of other countries of South and Central America, became victims and consumers of this multi-national business of the production and distribution of many illicit drugs, especially cocaine.

"The whole country of Colombia, especially Medellín, became an epicenter of the CIA cocaine drug traffic for years, beginning in the early 1980's. Approved by then-President Ronald Reagan, the profits were to be used to covertly combat communism and anti-American activities in South America, Central America and the world. It is ironic that a country known for 'protection of freedom' became the ultimate country for enslavement of the people."

Much of the money was also used covertly for secret space programs, which had their beginnings with the corporate military complex of the United States, after World War II. Please read Insiders Reveal Secret Space Programs & Extraterrestrial Alliances, by Michael E. Salla, Ph.D.

Father Gabriel continued, "Colombia was a simple country with family values prior to the drug cartels of the coca trade. Respect for life and the cultivation of nature for clean water, wholesome food and housing, and concern for the planet's bounty were a part of every Colombian's life."

Father Gabriel became emotional, saying, "Most of the raw coca leaves were harvested and brought from Bolivia, Ecuador and Peru to be processed here in Colombia, but was later cultivated in Colombia. Pablo Escobar was picked by the CIA to lead cocaine business, trade and production in Medellín. He became one of the most infamous and powerful men in South America, establishing the Medellín cartel and moving billions of dollars in and out of the country. Pablo started out using half of his profits to build schools and hospitals, bringing Colombia out of third world status. But, the corruption of the illicit drug trade would later bring violence, murder, and scandal to the once peaceful country and its people.

"I, and my brothers and sisters, are leading the movement to change Colombia and other Latin American countries, to reverse the damage done to our people, and help them to become clean from drugs, alcohol, violence and sexual troubles that began because of the drug wars still going on today," added Father Gabriel.

Chapter 14 - Another Visit to Santa Elena

The Three Fathers would start their day with meditation at 5 AM, followed by mass at 6 AM. We would all then gather at 8:30 AM at the table in the dining room beside the kitchen for breakfast, served by Maria, who was in charge of the kitchen and washing of bedding and clothes. By 9 AM, we would be on the road heading down the mountain in the white Volkswagen Passat to the main road, Avenida Oriental, to the headquarters of the Hogares Claret.

On one visit to Santa Elena, we entered a cab at the downtown headquarters to drive up to the Hogares Claret of the adults in the mountainside southeast of Medellín. For 35 minutes, through heavy traffic, we climbed up the Andes mountains which surrounded Medellín. The road became more narrow with less traffic, and eventually turned to dirt with fences and farms on both sides. Cows were grazing and horses galloping in the pastures and slopes to the right of the road. It was a green paradise above the city.

La Cierra Santa Elena of the Hogares Claret, high in the mountains above Medellín, is where the adult male population live and are treated with all the modalities of healing therapy.

We first visited with the employees, where I was again introduced and treated with the respect of a foreign dignitary. I was given an tour of the facilities while Padre Gabriel attended another leadership meeting.

I was escorted through all the offices on the first floor, then taken through a large modern kitchen with several cooks and assistants, busily cleaning up after breakfast. They all smiled and greeted me with "buenos dias," and each wanted to show me what they were doing. There were several other cooks preparing lunch (almuerzo), vegetable soup, rice, chicken, and fruit plates. I saw a pot filled with corn, fruit and sugar being prepared so I asked what it was. The women preparing the pot answered, "A dulce (sweet) dessert." I nodded to show my understanding and said, "Ciao." The staff all repeated it after me, saying their goodbyes.

Next, we went outside the building in the back where many workers with construction helmets were busy planting trees and plants behind a fence. Many others were in the process of building horse barns and a larger building for group therapies which had some small rooms for refreshments and smaller groups, which overlooked the valley far below. The view inspired me, with all the pastures, small homes and farms growing tropical guava, papaya, banana trees and vegetable gardens in full view descending to the valley below.

We walked several hundred yards to a large multi-acre garden of "bird of paradise" flowers which were being cultivated, flourishing in full bloom. "Bird of paradise flowers are associated with liberty, freedom, magnificence and a higher life perspective, making it a perfect flower essence to stimulate the children's and adults' attitude," stated my guide. "So you make flower essences here in Santa Elena?" I questioned. "Yes," he said, "and we use many others, especially the Bach flower essences, mostly 'Rescue Remedy.'"

I remembered how as an obstetrician/gynecologist and physician, I had learned to use flower essences for emotional trauma with mothers and girls who had been abused and/or raped to quickly help them cope and overcome the savagery of these assaults. I marveled at how Father Gabriel had incorporated Flower Essence Therapy into the Hogares Claret to help heal the children from their traumatic emotional wounds. I walked away feeling freer, with a lighter step, after muzzling up to the flowers and smelling the scent of the beautiful "bird of paradise" flowers.

We rejoined Padre Gabriel, with the therapists going with us, at the conjoined facility where some seventy men, in treatment for addiction, abuse, and alcoholism, were in a group therapy meeting. They were all in a well-lit library, seated in a large circle of chairs.

Padre Gabriel asked if we could join them again as we had done on the previous visit, and with much happiness from the group, we entered and took seats next to the leaders of the group therapy. Padre Gabriel, who needed no introduction, gave a short dissertation, telling the entire group how much he loved them and honored them for the work they continued to do to improve their lives and become better men. He introduced me to the group as "Dr. Scott Werner," a medical doctor from the United States of North America, and allowed me to speak.

I introduced myself again and gave some of my background, which included being a doctor specializing in women's care, managing pregnancies, delivering babies, and doing surgery. I told them how I had learned Transcendental Meditation in the United States in 2006. I also told them of the dream about Maharishi in January 2011, where he was floating in the air above my bed saying, "Go to Fairfield and detox my people." That guided me to go to Fairfield, Iowa, to introduce a new detox for the people that removed chemicals and toxins which were being produced and used in the Monsanto farms producing genetically modified plants and experimental chemical fields surrounding the city and most of southeastern Iowa.

I then told them of the visit of St. Germaine, and the answer to the question of, "What can we do to overcome the high levels of toxins, radiation, petrochemicals and nanobots we are exposed to?" St. Germaine taught, "We need to evolve by creating and expanding our

DNA to 24 strands, putting it into 12 double helixes and braiding them into rope DNA, making our DNA stronger, invincible, indestructible, and impenetrable to all the environmental toxins, including radiation and nanobots."

I was inspired to say, "St. Germaine sent me to Colombia, to meet Father Gabriel and learn of the treatments and detoxing he has established in the Hogares Claret. You are the future of Colombia and the world. You have gone through your experiences to teach yourself how to overcome drug addictions, alcoholism, and problems of abuse and lack. Father Gabriel is giving you the methods and tools to become better human beings, beings of integrity, kindness, and love, reintegrating you back into society, to heal that society with your newfound love and knowledge. You are becoming socially adept, with control over your mind, emotions, body and spirit. This is the perfect environment of peace, love, and joy to heal your souls."

When I sat down, everyone in the room started clapping, including Father Gabriel. We completed the meeting with bear hugs and handshakes.

We then went down to the cafeteria where we were fed a lunch of baked chicken with herbs, rice and beans, fresh vegetables, and dessert of fruit, spices and sugar, which was delicious (it was the same fruit mixture which was being prepared in the kitchen by the happy ladies cooking earlier).

Camilo then reappeared and Father Gabriel told him to teach me about the Panchakarma area upstairs. *Pancha* means five and *karma* means soul-treatment. These therapies are done to detoxify the body, emotions, mental body and soul, according to Ayurvedic medicine. The building has been remodeled to accommodate the various treatments for the residents of the center, but also for visitors who can stay at the facility. Camilo, the Director of Panchakarma at the

Hogares Claret of Santa Elena, explained the five primary therapies used to balance and eliminate the damage to the doshas.

Virechana

Virechana is a treatment with herbs and essential oils, removing toxins and parasites from the liver, gallbladder, pancreas and intestinal tract.

A medicated purgation therapy, it removes Pitta toxins from the body that are accumulated in the liver and gallbladder, and completely cleanses the gastro-intestinal tract. It is a safe procedure without side effects, given each day, or every other day, for eight to fourteen days.

Benefits – Treats chronic fever, diabetes, asthma, skin disorders such as viral infections, nerve disorders such as paraplegia, hemiplegia, joint disorders, digestive disorders, constipation, hyperacidity, vitiligo, psoriasis, headaches, elephantiasis (parasites), gynecological disorders.

Vamana

Another one of the Panchakarma procedures, Vamana is a medicated emesis therapy which cleanses Kapha toxins collected in the body and decongests the respiratory tract. Daily treatments are administered to loosen and mobilize the toxins and to finally eliminate them. This therapy takes eight to ten days.

Benefits – Treats bronchial asthma, chronic allergies, hay fever, vitiligo, psoriasis, hyperacidity, chronic indigestion, nasal congestion, edema, obesity, psychological disorders, skin disorders.

Basti

Considered the mother of all treatments, Basti cleanses the accumulated toxins from all the 3 dochas, Vata, Pitta and Kapha, especially Vata toxins, through the colon. Basti is also highly beneficial as a rejuvenating treatment, especially in convalescent periods. Medicated oil or ghee and an herbal decoction are given as enema to clean the colon and increase the muscle tone. This procedure is usually applied for eight to thirty days, based on the medical condition of a person.

Benefits – Treats nervous conditions, hemiplegia, paraplegia, colitis, convalescence, cervical spondylosis, irritable bowel syndrome, constipation, digestive disorders, backache and sciatica, hepatomegaly and splenomegaly, obesity, piles (hemorrhoids), sexual debility and infertility.

Nasya

Nasya is the administration of medicated oil through the nose. It cleanses accumulated Kapha toxins from the head and neck region. This treatment is usually given for seven days. Based on the medical condition of a person, it can be given up to thirty days.

Benefits – Treats trigeminal neuralgia, Bell's Palsy, poor memory and eyesight, insomnia, excess mucus, hyper pigmentation in the face, pre-mature graying of hair, loss of clarity to voice, headaches of various origin, hemiplegia, loss of smell and taste, frozen shoulder, migraine, stiffness of the neck, nasal allergies, nasal polyps, neurological dysfunctions, paraplegia, sinusitis.

Raktamokshana

Raktamokshana is a very effective blood purification therapy in which carefully controlled removal of small quantities of blood is conducted to neutralize accumulated Pitta toxins of many blood-borne diseases.

Benefits – Treats allergies, skin disorders such as eczema, allergic dermatitis, tonsillitis, sciatica.

Chapter 15 - Hogares Claret de La Libertad

June 4, 2015

Again, the rain pattering on the roof at 4 AM woke me. I decided to meditate as my mind would not let me go back to sleep. As I stated my mantra and "Om" in my head, I immediately transcended to a place in the unified field I had never encountered. There were several universes swirling in the distance, revolving around an immense energy of golden-white light.

A golden-white being appeared, whose golden energy was mainly expressed from the heart, with intense white energy surrounding the entire human-appearing body. It was dressed in a garment of gold with an apron of blue, white and gold crystalline energy. Intensely shining blue eyes with several revolving vortices pierced my soul, revealing my every thought. White light emanated from the third eye forward and upward with a golden fire of light surrounding the entire head, like golden light flowing hair, energetically moving and flowing, extending down past the shoulders and down the back.

I thought, "Who is this?" And I heard in my mind, "I am the Great Divine Director, and I have come to you with a message. You have been brought to this place, in the center of an ever-expanding universe, to be shown the magnificence and Love of God.

"All humanity is expressing the creative energy and omnipresence and omnificence of the universe. Terrestrial humans are on the verge of their continuing evolution on earth, and are to be taught of the vibratory Ascension, which will take place en masse on the earth for those humans who are ready to become free from the heavier vibrations of the third dimension, within the end of this generation coming to the earth now. You will be guided and protected by the golden Light of God.

"You are to take this message to the earth to prepare and teach of the evolution of the DNA and the Ascension to this generation of human beings, and those of previous generations who will listen."

He then took me to a viewpoint of the energies emerging and emanating from the golden white plasma and photonic mass of energy central to the universe. "This is the Great Central Sun, whose energy is nourishing and bathing the universe and the earth with Love and Light in vast quantities, helping with this evolution." I could hear the Divine Director of Golden Light say telepathically, to my mind and every cell in my body, "It is time, the earth will soon receive her Paradisiacal Glory. Prepare and teach the people."

He then faced me, and I was then filled with the photonic and plasma energy streaming with the golden-white light flowing from this magnificent being, bringing love, joy, compassion, and ecstasy into my soul.

I awoke with the celebration of the Mass beginning from the other room. It was 6:05 AM.

I pulled the sheets and blanket neatly up to the pillows, with the voice of my Grandma June Nicoles speaking to me, "You make your bed, like you make your day." I remembered she always taught me, "When the day starts out making a neat tidy bed, the day will be neat and tidy and productive." So I pulled up the comforter and tucked it neatly under and over the pillows.

I shaved, making sure every whisker was removed, splashed cold water on and under my eyes and mouth, dried my face with a fresh white towel Maria had left for me, then walked out to call Vicki on

Facetime, telling her about the amazing spiritual experience with the Great Divine Director.

This morning we sat down to a grand breakfast again of poached eggs, fresh papaya and mangos.

I love fresh organic papaya as it was a key part of the regimen of pineapple, passion fruit and papaya which healed my pancreas after a stone lodged into my "ampulla of Vater" (the opening of the combined bile and pancreatic duct into the duodenum, or first part of the small intestine).

The stone blocked the flow of pancreatic juices combined with bile, regurgitating the digestive mixture back up into my pancreas and gallbladder, causing cholecyctitis/pancreatitis, which instead of digesting my food in the small intestine, started digestion of my pancreatic cells including the "islets of Langerhans" or insulin-producing cells.

I remembered how I had almost died from the pancreatitis, but through the guidance of the healing Masters, I flew to the Big Island of Hawaii to heal with the volcanic energy of creation emanating from the still-active volcano, Mauna Loa, and by eating papaya, pineapple and passion fruit with their enzymes to dissolve the stone and vibrate its passage out of the ampulla of Vater, into the duodenum and out the small intestines to the colon and out of my body.

As I remembered these thoughts, Father Gabriel said, "Buenos dias, Dr. Scott," in his usual happy state. I greeted him back, as well as the other Fathers as they each greeted me with, "Buenos dias, Doctor Scott." I told them all briefly of my dream and they nodded approvingly with sparkles in their eyes, telling me how wonderful it was to have dreams such as these.

I left the house with The Three Fathers at 9 AM to go to another one of the houses of Hogares Claret, after another perfect breakfast made with love by Maria.

Hogares Claret de la Libertad in the northwest pueblo of San Cristobal of Medellín houses children 12-18 years old. These children, who matriculate into the Hogares, have been living in the streets since they were very small. Some walked away from overcrowded orphanages when there was nothing to eat. They have been used and abused, becoming prostitutes, sex slaves, and then drug addicts and alcoholics, to take away the pain and emotional negativity. They hear about Father Gabriel and the wonderful programs offered at the Hogares Claret, and ask to be taken off the streets so they can improve their lives.

Most haven't seen their parents in years, or have been orphans. Many have been using inhalants or other drugs for years. Sexual abuse is very common for making money and getting the basics of food and water. Shelter on the streets is hard to come by and the homeless are very territorial. Some have cardboard boxes, some just a sheet of metal for a slide, to remove the water. Most have nothing as any material can be stolen as they sleep. The Hogares Claret offers protection, shelter, food and clean water, and most of all, safety.

All substance abuse treatment is explained, taught and offered, including treatment for cocaine alkaloid, alcohol, marijuana, and perico (cocaine in all its forms). The word perico "parrot" in English is used because the cocaine goes up the nose and it gives you a sting like a parrot's bite. There is also treatment for cocaine paste, also known as coca paste, paco, pasta base or basuco in South America, short for pasta de cocaína (cocaine paste) or pasta base de cocaína, coca pegante inhalants, pasta decoca basuco, and alcoholism. Many also need treatment for amphetamines, used to stay awake so they are not robbed in their sleep. Below are some of the combinations described to me by the children:

THC + basuco = diablo

THC + coca = angel

Heroin + coca = paco

Alcohol is used by many of the street children as an emotional numbing agent and usually during sexual abuse and penetration.

Hogares Claret Treatments and Philosophy:

Free Choice: First, get the child involved. The child is always given the choice.

The Phases of treatment: Entrance—treatment and progress—graduation and certificates.

- Identification of birth, parents, age, home, pueblo if available
- Elaboration or evaluation of all addictive substances, variable abuse and psychological damage
- Consultation with various psychologists, treatment facilities, and integration into Hogares Claret
- Continued evaluation of progress
- Graduation when completing treatments and/or schooling for each grade (developing self-esteem)

Benefits of Hogares Claret

- Protection…participation…education…health-life
- Overcoming issues of the health, life, and overcoming addictive behaviors.
- Providing a reason for existence.
- Health…psychological evaluation…medications, flower essences, and herbs, if needed
- Good nutrition…three nutritious meals a day and healthy snacks

- Social integration…work and play every day…professional family protection
- Instructions in work techniques and school studies, both primary and secondary
- Professors of meditation are on staff, providing Transcendental Meditation mainly but other methods are available. Meditation is provided for all students, but all religious beliefs are protected and encouraged: Catholic, Pentecostal, Protestant, etc.

Overview of Services

General services: Housing, bedding, self-care including laundry, showers, dental and oral health. The children are responsibly taught and do their own laundry, cleaning of bathrooms and showers. The children are involved and responsible for group areas and personal space including making their bed every day.

Integration into society: Getting the children integrated into family, social situations and teachings.

Interviews and evaluation: Planning treatments, starting treatments, evaluating treatments and progress counseling… evaluation…identification…additional counseling as needed then slowly reintegrating into society. Put them back into society, sane, healthy, and sober.

After graduation (usually 18 years old or more if needed) and integration into work or school, the Hogares Claret continue to contact with site or home visits, daily or weekly telephone calls and general support.

The goal is to transition from institutional therapy to the therapeutic community and then to independent living. They are always encouraged to be a part of the Hogares Claret community and participate with social events, teach classes and assist with therapy.

This is part of the Logotherapy of Viktor Frankl, or self-actualization. It is human, holistic, systemic and integrated with logic, broad thinking and individualization.

The child has choice during the entire process, but learns very early in treatment that there are consequences of free will.

The process restores to the child lost values, lost basic human rights, the ability to live with freedom, and increased faith, trust and lust for life.

Hogares Clarets Mission:

1. Accompanying the people or children through the process of reintegration into society and reformation of value through the project of life and Transcendental Meditation.

2. Basic education in consciousness, Christian family values, Colombian scouts, spiritual companionship.

Hogares Clarets Goals and Methods:

1. Comprehensive therapy:

- Remove blockages through group therapies
- Interviews in groups and individual counseling
- Tutorials
- Crisis intervention
- Re-formation of self and education
- Ensembles of small groups or families: not taking the place of parental rights

- Democratic games: teaching society and political analysis lessons
- Group therapies: integrating child into community interaction
- Confrontation therapies: teaching about misbehavior and regression
- Marathon therapy for one week to integrate persistence rewards
- Horse and animal therapy, used to remove emotional trauma

2. **Academic Studies:**

- Primary and secondary…university…upper studies…virtual education
- Cultural education including integration of tolerance of different belief systems
- Games and fun: scouts…art…music…sports
- Formative assessment is a range of formal and informal assessment procedures conducted by teachers during the learning process in order to modify teaching and learning activities to improve student attainment.

3. **Sexuality/psychological health:** Reintegration of self worth and healthy sexuality. Preventive teaching of sexual abstinence is the practice of refraining from all aspects of sexual activity for medical, psychological, legal and social reasons, using Transcendental Meditation as a resource.

4. **Family/school:** Integrating the students in the Hogares Claret back into a family environment if possible, or using the students themselves in teaching the importance of family values.

5. **Civil obedience and integration into society:**

- Boy Scouts and Girl Scouts teaching the values of scouting, fun and service

- Prevention of disasters or recognizing difficulties prior to disasters to prevent them
- Preparation for life and values: teaching each child values of family, community, and being a good citizen

6. Spiritual development:

- Yoga or control of the mind and body: In yoga, asana refers both to the place and state of mind, in which a practitioner (yogi if male, yogini if female) sits and the positioning of the body. Most of the children in Hogares Claret are taught to meditate sitting upright, either with the legs crossed or sitting in a chair with both feet planted on the floor facing forward.
- Transcendental Meditation: Each child is taught traditional Transcendental Meditation with a mantra and exact methods to accomplish sound meditative awareness.

Chapter 16 - Hogares Claret Caldas

Afternoon, June 4, 2015

We traveled to another home of Hogares Claret in Caldas, a small community in the mountains south of Medellín.

The pueblo of Caldas was a city with extreme poverty. The roads were full of potholes. Trash seemed abundant. Many people were just hanging out in the streets.

We made a left turn going up an even more damaged street along a stream coming down off the mountain. Another left took us to a locked gate; we honked the horn and nobody came. I looked closer at the lock of the gate and it looked as if it was open, so I asked the driver Alex's permission to get out of the van.

"Of course," he said in Spanish.

I got out of the van and easily opened the gate. The driver was very surprised that the gate was open. I asked if I should stay outside to close the gate as he drove past, but he said people inside would lock the gate back up.

As we entered the courtyard, I could see several dozen young men all dressed in blue pants and red shirts playing with a soccer ball, up and down an elongated green grass field. We pulled up to a white building with a large covered carport and got out of the van.

Several of the young men approached the van and looked at me with questions and big eyes. "Who are you?" they asked. When I answered, "Doctor Scott," they asked if I was there to do physical examinations. I told them "No, I'm here just to observe you and see the facility where you are living." They all laughed and smiled and asked me to come with them and they quickly grabbed my hands and led me to each one of their rooms, each showing me their bunk, and then to another building which appeared to be another dorm at the facility.

In this building they showed me that there was a Bobcat dorm with 10 bunk beds for 20 boys, a Bears dorm with the same number of bunk beds and 20 boys, and a Lions dorm which also had 10 bunk beds for 20 boys. Each was very clean and all beds were made. Clothing, towels, and cleaning items were not seen as they all had been put away in their places, and the boys were all proud to show me their spaces.

Next, they took me to an art room where there were many materials, paints, and leather pieces available for making different forms of art and handicrafts.

After the art room, they led me a conference area where they could sit and have group meetings. Each boy seemed to have a joyful youthfulness with and about him; some seemed almost to be hyperactive, and others internally contemplative. All of them seemed very happy to be at the facility and pleased that I was visiting with them. As I asked them about their stories and how they had found Hogares Claret, they were very open to tell me about their experiences living in the streets and how happy they were to make the decision and transition to come to Hogares Claret.

One of the boys appeared to have several old burns with scarring on his neck, face, arms and legs. He told a story of having been lit on fire after a gasoline accident. He said he felt so ugly when he was on the streets that he didn't feel worthy to live. While living at the Hogares Claret Foundation, he learned that his life had purpose and meaning and he was grateful and happy to be alive. Now it didn't matter how he looked on the outside because he felt happy on the inside.

The leaders called all the boys together underneath the covered carport area near the kitchen and eating facilities. They all made a line in front of a window where they were to be served a beverage and a snack. Then, they all crowded around me, putting me at the front of the line, trying to make sure I was treated as their guest. All the boys laughed and smiled at me and wanted me to feel at home.

After fruit juice, fruit and a grain snack they called "cannoli" were gone, it started to sprinkle drops of rain, and the leaders called everyone into the large carport where there were about 80 chairs. We all sat down to listen to the leaders. The ten leaders introduced me as Doctor Scott and called on several of the boys to tell me their stories.

One handsome young man, about 13 years old, talked about how he had been living in the streets since he was very young, four or five years old. He couldn't remember his mother or his father ever being there, but he knew he had parents. He lived for several years in the streets with a handler, or pimp, who set him up with men where he was used for sex. He began to use inhalants to subdue and numb his negative emotions. Other drugs were too expensive to use and his owner collected all the monies he earned, so he never had anything to call his own. This went on for five more long years, never having stability or a stable shelter, or a good meal to eat.

He stated with a wide smile, "One rainy day, Father Gabriel saw me from his car, stepped out into the rain, and his caring compassionate smile captivated me. He saved my life by stopping and inviting me to join the foundation of Hogares Claret. Being a part of Hogares Claret made my life worth living and I started to have meaning and purpose in my life. Now, I am free of all drugs and any desire to use them. I know I am loved and have purpose."

Another young man stood and started telling a similar story, but much more vivid, and several of the children stated he was making it up. (They called him mentiroso or liar in English.) It came up during the discussion that he felt very ugly and no one wanted to be with him, not even for his body. He had come to the foundation from the streets at 10 years old, without any family, friends, or love.

The foundation had accepted him and helped him to see there was more to life than living in the streets. At the end of his confessions, he apologized for lying about some of his story, and asked me to forgive him, and I immediately stated, "I forgive you and never judged you."

He immediately ran over to me, hugging me tightly for a long time, with big tears running down his cheeks and saying, "I love you Doctor Scott. Thank you for coming to see me."

I immediately spoke to the group while this beautiful young man, José, held me tight. "Everyone wants to fit in. Everyone desires to be loved and have a place and purpose in this world. Everyone dreams to be a part of making this world a better place, filled with love and purpose. I believe we can do this. I believe you can change the world by changing you. To make the world change, I must change. To make the world better, I must become better.

"You are the leaders of this better world, by becoming leaders, being teachers, being somebody who can contribute to the community." I told José, still clinging to my waist, "As you grow, learn, and become a mentor, a father, and a leader, learning the truth and telling the truth is more important than any fantasy you could conjure up, and the truth shall make you free."

I told the group the story of one of my children from a previous marriage, who had started using drugs at the age of 13 and how he dropped out of school in the eighth grade. As a father, I had tried everything to get him to go back to school, including sitting with him for three months in his classroom to ensure that he made something out of his life. I told them how he had tested earlier in life in school down in Phoenix, Arizona, as a genius and in the third, fourth and fifth grades he had been accepted into an accelerated school for exceptional children. He excelled in the accelerated programs for learning during his elementary education because of his mental abilities. When we moved to a small town in Utah, where he was not as stimulated with education, he turned to drugs, being bored with life, thinking life had passed him by. I told them that for 12 years he had been in and out of detention and later incarcerated in the adult jail system, due to his drug use, mainly marijuana. He was not a bad young man, but very disillusioned and lost.

Finally, I helped him move to Las Vegas, Nevada, to start a new life, away from the harmful influences that he had in Utah. He started out making pizzas at a pizza business and within six months became the manager, due to his intelligence and resourcefulness.

I started to tear up and get emotional. Becoming the manager helped with his self-confidence and self-esteem. He also developed self-love and opened up to the possibilities of marriage and a family. I told them he now lives in Denver, Colorado, with the girl of his dreams and is very happy in his life.

I could see visibly that the story moved all of these young men. The story I told them moved me to tears because it was so close to my own heart, and there were several times while I told the story that I broke down and couldn't keep the tears from flowing. I told them how important it was that they were safe with the foundation at this moment in their lives, that it would turn their lives around to opportunities and possibilities that they could never have imagined before. I told them that the world is a safe place when you know that you are loved, have value, and can make a difference to make the world a better place.

When I finished, several other boys told their stories, being very honest and open. After the meeting, many of them surrounded me wanting to shake my hand and give hugs of gratitude and love. José stayed close by, still connected and desiring interaction.

After about an hour of talking with them, the informal gathering was finished with my giving a blessing for all of them. I stated, "In the name of the Father, the Son and the Holy Spirit, I bless each of you with health, strong minds and bodies, knowing that you are loved and have purpose, to bless and make this world a paradise. I bless you with strength to lead others, become the teachers of the next generation, helping them to also create a happier, more loving and beautiful world, Amen." The leaders and students all got up from their seats and all surrounded me with a big group hug.

Several children ran out on the grass and started kicking a soccer ball around. About 40 children continued to surround us as we said our goodbyes and got back into the van.

As we drove out the gate, which still hadn't been locked, I knew we were leaving the children in good hands. I could still feel the love and clarity of the children as we drove back to the main offices of Hogares Claret. The sensation of love and peace the children and leaders felt in Hogares Claret spilled over into my own soul.

Chapter 17 - The Dream

June 5, 2015

I awoke with the sounds of the Padres reciting their morning prayers and Mass, and jumped out of bed because I thought I had overslept. I hurriedly put on my clothes, made my bed, shaved and showered, making myself presentable for the day and hurried out the door of my room. It was only 5:30 AM, and breakfast wouldn't be served for another three hours.

I laughed at myself, and it was wonderful feeling so fresh and alive. I had only been in Colombia for five days, but the fresh organic food, pristine water and cool mountain air was having a healing effect on my body and mind. I felt a bliss and vitality gaining strength within my system.

I retired back in my room and began to meditate and pray, just like the priests in the other room.

I fell back to sleep and had a dream of another life, in the past, where I had been a priest in Europe. I was assisting the widows and orphans after a terrible war had ravaged the land and taken the lives of the fathers and many of the women. In this dream, the church was crowded with straw-filled beds that went out to the pews, and women and children were everywhere. I was in charge of feeding them and giving them shelter and water, the basics of life.

Every day, I would awake early and lead several of the children to gather eggs, collect berries and tend to the garden, grind flour and help to make bread for breakfast. The whole day was spent fulfilling the basic needs of the people under my care. At the end of each day, I would be exhausted, yet filled with the Love of God.

In the dream, the mothers and children were in a constant state of gratitude, and the feelings behind the dream let me know the Three Fathers were an inspired part of healing the abandoned, disposable ones of Colombia and other countries in South America.

Chapter 18 - Mira Flores

I awoke from the dream hearing the Fathers gathering for breakfast. I quickly washed my face and joined them.

Maria, as usual, made a marvelous breakfast with potato cakes and fried eggs.

Father Gabriel commented that I had slept in and asked if I was okay. I told him about the dream and he and the other Fathers smiled approvingly. Father Gabriel stated, "You were one of us in a past life and are becoming one with us in this life."

We finished up breakfast, brushed our teeth and headed down the familiar path, with flowers of every color seeming brighter today. The white Volkswagen had been cleaned and was waiting for us to drive down the mountain.

I laughed with joy.

Today we traveled to the main offices of the Hogares Claret in downtown Medellín. George, one of the directors, met me and we traveled by publico, a van-like taxi, up the mountain to a community called Mira Flores, several miles above Medellín.

It was quite a ride up steep roads with very sharp turns. There were several men stationed along the side of the road, controlling the movement of traffic and helping us move safely up the mountain. The roads were very narrow, with many parked cars on both sides making the road even more narrow. The men directed the cars and large trucks, helping them even move backward and forward because there were many sharp, blind turns going up and down these narrow roads, so they could drive the roads more safely. As we passed these men, George would give them coins of money as we traveled up the highway. I asked George if this was common. He stated many of the men had lost their jobs and they wanted to help the community by preventing accidents and help traffic flow more easily. It wasn't required to pay the individuals, but Father Gabriel insisted on paying coins to the drivers and also to the men attending the roads. Employees of Hogares Claret were distributed coins for each trip.

When we approached a building with a parking lot and a large gate out front, George had the taxi driver honk and several girls dressed in colorful clothes ran down to the gate. As the gate was opened, George said, "We are at the Mira Flores Hogares Claret, home for teenage girls."

The girls greeting us at the gate were all dressed in modern, colorful street clothes, which were very pleasant to look at. I learned that this program housed 58 young girls, and several older girls in a separate building who had finished the programs of Hogares Claret and were attending college or professional schools. The older girls stayed in little apartments, separate, but still connected with the facilities for the younger girls.

I noticed one of the girls who greeted us at the gate had undergone surgery for a "hair-lip" from birth. She was very happy and verbally very excited to see us. I could tell she knew George and liked him a lot. She was the only one who continued with us to the main offices next to the dorms. The other girls just smiled and giggled, then went back to their activities.

George and I entered the office complex quickly. We walked to an area outside the offices of the leaders where we signed into a ledger book, which was customary for visitors entering any controlled area. The Hogares were fenced in and locked up as a protection to prevent outsiders from entering and leaving with the children, and also to control any unwanted visitors from entering the compounds and causing trouble.

George then led me into the main offices and introduced me to all the workers and the director of the facility for the girls. Everyone in the offices acted very excited that an American doctor was interested in what they were doing.

I was given a tour by the director Natalia Munoz, who takes care of and leads all of the employees and social workers at the facility in Mira Flores.

All the girls in the facility were wearing makeup that day and dressed in regular day clothes. I asked, "Why are the girls not in uniforms like all the boys at the other facilities?" Natalia answered, "Once a week, the girls dress up and wear makeup as if they are living in normal homes in the outside world. Unlike the boys, each has a bed, bathroom facilities, and a private area to dress and prepare themselves for the day." Natalia continued to show me all the different facilities for these girls, whose ages were from 11 to 18 years of age. She stated, "Once the girls start going through puberty, they are advanced to this facility."

After showing me all the facilities, including areas for art and other creative projects, Natalia took me to another building in the front where older girls who had completed the program and secondary high school were housed. While these girls were attending higher education at various colleges and trade schools, they could live there and complete their education. In this building, the girls were free to come and go as they pleased, not needing the restrictions of the girls who were still under-aged and needing protection.

Natalia then described, "Just like the boys become Cub Scouts and Boy Scouts, the girls become Girl Scouts, which helps with social and group development and physical activity and games for the girls. Every year, the girls also sell Colombian Girl Scout cookies."

Natalia moved us to an outdoor section where there were several log obstacles, tires and play areas that were used to develop balance, physical stability and strength.

George gathered the girls out in the courtyard to give a short motivational speech at the top of the stairs. After George spoke, he introduced me and I gave a spontaneous short talk about the importance of the girls' decisions to be at the Hogares Claret. I told them that they were in very good hands and all their instructors were very qualified to help them get through their teenage years.

I told them, "It is very important to prepare yourselves for the future. I have worked with girls and women as an obstetrician, a woman doctor, delivering many babies. Some from very young mothers. That work prepared me to write the book I am writing about the wonderful opportunities Father Gabriel has created for you to develop your lives and prepare you for the future."

I spoke about how my training as a medical doctor and obstetrician gave me the desire to help the world, and if the women having the babies were healthier, better prepared to be mothers, and happier, the babies would be healthier and happier too, creating a generation of happy, healthy humans.

I told them how I would teach the women to send love each day to their babies prior to birth, to be happy, pray for the perfection of their developing children in the womb, play classical music, feed themselves healthy organic food, have happy and joyful thoughts, and to avoid contention in any form.

If the father was a poor influence, with bad habits such as drug use or being contentious in any form, I told them to leave and be in a better environment so the babies would be born in a more content, joyful and healthier, happier environment.

I also told them how important it is to keep their bodies clean and pure from drugs, sexually transmitted disease, bad foods, alcohol and substances that would damage their bodies. I told them that the Hogares Claret were set up with a design which would give them all the tools and understanding they would need to become healthy adults and women, and later, mothers. I encouraged them to utilize their time and efforts in the Hogares Claret to get the most out of the program while they are here.

Once I finished my little speech, several girls gathered around me, asking questions about me and my family. I told them that I had 10 children and they were very surprised. They asked if the children were from various women. I explained that I had been married for 23 ½ years to my first wife, having had and raised five children with her. I divorced from my first wife because we had many differences, especially about the raising of our children. Later, I married my current wife, Vicki. She had three children from her previous marriage, whom I helped raise, and we had two children together, making ten children in all. Vicki and I had the same values and ideas about teaching and raising children, which was a great blessing.

The girls were very interested in me speaking to them in English, though their proficiency was just basic words. I continued speaking in Spanish and asked them about an immunization called "Gardasil," a quadravalent vaccination containing attenuated (weakened) human papilloma virus type 6, 11, 16 and 18. It is an immunization given to young girls, usually between 13-15 years old, for the prevention of cervical cancer. Many of the girls knew of this immunization and it had been given to them. All they knew was they had to receive the immunization for STD's. They didn't understand that it possibly only prevents one viral type of several infectious types of STD's, human papilloma virus, which causes cervical and possibly uterine and vaginal cancer as well. I discussed with them that there are many other types of sexually transmitted diseases and that monogamy, with one partner who also chooses monogamy, is the only way to avoid these diseases.

They asked if I was monogamous and I answered them saying, "When I married at the age of 21, I was a virgin and my new wife was the only one I had sex with." Many of the girls giggled as I continued, "When I was divorced, at the age of 45, I still had only been with my first wife. When I remarried, to Vicki, we chose to care for each other and love and cherish each other, until death do us part. We committed to each other to be faithful sexually, also."

They all seemed satisfied with my answers to their questions and were continuing with more questions, when the leaders called us to lunch.

We ate lunch consisting of a bowl of bean soup, seasoned chicken, rice, a fried platano and a dessert of sweet corn in the juices of the corn and a sugar fruity candy, which was all very tasty together.

The leaders were very open to questions and one of my main questions was, "How successful is this program?" They were very proud to tell me that all the girls who attended the foundation and participated in all of the programs, including meditation, had a success rate of 98%. This particular school for the girls was opened in 1990.

There were several girls attending the local University and other schools of higher education who had asked to stay on with the foundation, using it as their home base. They had separate facilities in the front apartment complex, which was inside the compound but toward the front. They had a separate exit and entrance to go to school and to other activities without being locked in at night. Some of these older girls were present, and were excited to show me their small apartments in the building next to the street. Each one had separate rooms and an area to cook their own meals. I noticed each room had a different musical instrument, which the girls had been trained to play proficiently. One girl told me, "Musical training is available and taught to each girl at this facility. Each one of us chose an instrument and were also trained in voice and singing." I was told they were welcome to eat with the other girls and participate with younger girls, but their main focus should be on their education.

We went to another building, which was more like studio apartments, with separate apartments for each girl providing them their own space. They had computers and books, artwork which they had created, and musical instruments for their use. Most of these girls had outside jobs and paid for their apartments. They were still very connected to Hogares Claret. I was so impressed.

All of these young women were very happy and well-adjusted human beings. I could see that the successful young women who completed the program were integrated into society in almost better circumstances than most of those who had not been out in the streets, but had grown up in families. There was such a feeling of camaraderie, joy, bliss, and sense of family in the Hogares Claret. Each of these girls continued meditating, which has been shown in multiple double-blind studies to be a source of bliss, joy, and peace. Meditation has also been shown to be a source of health and longevity. We exited the apartments and walked back up to the director's office.

The girls were enjoying outside activities, but, seeing us coming back up the hill, asked if George would sing to them. One of the girls provided a guitar to George and he started singing familiar American pop music, but in Spanish. I was able to join in and sing as I knew the tunes and recognized the lyrics. The girls were very impressed with our singing together and harmonizing. We sang about five songs, then the director said to wrap up the concert.

We gathered up our bags, with the girls surrounding us, saying their goodbyes and thanking us for coming to serenade them. The gate opened and we exited the facility to find a small yellow cab waiting to take us back to the main headquarters down in Medellín.

We arrived at 4:45 PM, which is when Father Gabriel completed his business at the headquarters, said his goodbyes to the staff and gave them instructions for the following day. Then, the Three Fathers and I gathered together in the white Volkswagen, traveled back up to the compound for an hour of meditation, a wonderful dinner prepared by Maria, planned and prepared for the next day, and then went to bed for a restful night's sleep.

Chapter 19 - The Day in the Forest

June 6, 2015

At breakfast this morning, Father Gabriel pulled me aside and asked if I would go with Juan to see Medellín. He said, "You look like you need some recreation and time off, as you worked very hard this week. I planned for you to spend the day, for a holiday, seeing the countryside and other beautiful aspects of Medellín."

Maria had also taken the day off, so Father Gabriel buttered the toast, fried the eggs, and prepared the morning coffee. The other Fathers had spent the night at other locations, so it was just Father Gabriel and me that morning for breakfast.

As the two of us ate, Father Gabriel had many questions for me. He asked, "Do you enjoy teaching at the Maharishi University of Management there in Fairfield, Iowa?" I looked at him in bewilderment and replied, "I have never given the indication that I was a professor, or even involved with Maharishi's University of Management. St. Germaine and Monica Tovar made the arrangements for me to come to Colombia. I am a private person, divinely inspired to come and visit with you and write a book about the wondrous things you are doing here in Colombia, other countries in South America and Central America."

Father Gabriel laughed out loud and looked surprised, just like he had opened the best present he had ever received. He said, laughing, "I thought the University had sent you. What made you decide to come so far, clear to Colombia to see me?"

So I told him the story of how in January, 2011, Maharishi had come to me in a dream telling me to go to Fairfield, Iowa, and "detox his people." I added, "The same morning Maharishi appeared, a woman who lived in Fairfield, whom I had helped to detox and lose weight, called me on the phone with the proposition that I come and help 18 of her friends to lose weight and detox. They were willing to pay $100 each and fly me to Fairfield to teach them and do intuitive readings on them."

I then told Father Gabriel, "I followed the spirit and made plans to go to Fairfield, arriving in May 2011. I flew into Des Moines, drove to Fairfield and stayed at the home of Jeffrey Smith, author of *The Seeds of Deception and Genetic Roulette.* During the day I would give intuitive readings to the people in Fairfield and also give lectures on detoxing. Many who belonged to the Transcendental Meditation movement, who had heard of me by word-of-mouth, also desired intuitive readings, so I continued working hard doing two intuitive readings every hour, for 10-12 hours a day. I put the people on herbs and detoxing protocols particular to their situation, health and already diagnosed diseases.

"Many of the people had neurologic illnesses, including Parkinson's disease, Parkinson's life illnesses, multiple sclerosis, Lou Gehrig's disease, early dementia, Alzheimer's disease and other disorders of the brain and nervous system, including cancers and tumors. There were also many who had various liver diseases, and one man had total liver shutdown and failure and was dying. During the intuitive readings I used faith healing, blessings, toning, Reiki healing, touch therapy, essential oils and homeopathic remedies. Several people had spontaneous regression of their ailments (miracles).

"I traveled to a house where several people had asked me to go. This was the home of the man with severe liver failure, who was lying down on a cot, dying and barely breathing. His skin appeared greenish-yellow, from the yellow jaundice and bile retained in his body. I asked him, 'Do you have the faith to heal?' He told me, 'I want to live. I know you can help me.' So I laid my hands on his head and said, 'By the power of the ascended Masters, Jesus and the holy healing angels, I Bless your body to heal and receive health, vitality, energy and strength to heal your liver from the Light of God, so you will be able to complete your life purpose here upon the earth. I seal this blessing upon you, in the name of Jesus Christ, Amen.' After giving him the blessing and touch therapy, I was told to "tone," or send loving sounds for healing from God to his body and liver. I proceeded to intonate sounds with my voice starting with the Om, 528 hertz, key of F, for the heart chakra, making the infinity sign with my hands. I moved down to the solar plexus, intonating the sound of the key of E, resonating Ongga, and using the hand gestures of Alpha and Omega. I moved down into his sacral plexus, intonating the sound of the D note, using the vowels, Ah, Eh, Aye, Oh, Ooh, Ee, touching the five fingers with each vowel, and repeating them seven times. I moved down into his root chakra delivering the intonation of the key of C, with a deep glutteral Oonggaaah. I moved up into his throat chakra with the key of G and the intonation of I and Meeee.

"This man was very moved by what the healing Masters and angels had done for him. He wanted to get up from his deathbed and hug me, which he did. We sat and talked for about an hour, his voice strong and clear. I knew a miracle had happened in this man's life."

Father Gabriel and I talked intimately and frankly of the many experiences and many, many miracles which had happened in both of our lives. We agreed that we were very blessed to have Christ participate in the many healings and miracles.

Father Gabriel then called a cab to take me to where Juan was waiting to take me on a tour of the city and the area surrounding

Medellín. Father Gabriel paid for the cab, insisting I was his guest, again laughing about my origins.

The cab dropped me at a local train station. Juan had arranged that we travel by train and cable car throughout the city. There were trains, busses and several cable cars going up the Andes Mountains surrounding Medellín. We rode the train and stopped to get on a cable car. The ride up on the cable car took us over several hills, seeing the various barrios of the city from spectacular heights. Juan described each area and gave me the history of what he knew of Medellín. Juan had actually been working as the director of scouting in Colombia, in the capital of Bogotá, when Father Gabriel had asked him to direct the scouting program in the main offices of Hogares Claret. He had only been in Medellín for a month and his wife and children were still living in Bogotá. So we were actually both seeing many parts of the city for the first time.

We traveled by another train to the opposite side of the city, where we boarded yet another cable car, traveling up over yet another beautiful barrio, further up the mountain to a beautiful rain forest with multiple varieties of beautiful tropical trees, green as far as the eye could see. After several miles we arrived at the top, exited the cable car and walked to a beautiful dining area among the trees to eat lunch. Juan had been told by Father Gabriel to pay for the tour and lunch. It was a little cool on top of this mountain and I was glad I had brought my jacket. I ordered a warm soup and hot meal, even though the sun was shining in this equatorial national park. Juan stated we were over 10,000 feet in elevation.

Juan and I walked on a short trail on top of the mountain. It was a fairly large plateau and there were roads coming up from the opposite side of the mountain across from the city. He described that he had spent most of his adulthood working for the Boy Scouts of

Colombia in Bogotá. Father Gabriel had invited him to work with the Boy Scouts of Colombia in Medellín asking that he perfect the program in Medellín and other cities of the Hogares Claret.

After spending an hour and a half in this beautiful national forest of Colombia, we arrived back at the cable car and descended back into the valley.

When we arrived back at the original station where we boarded the train, Juan asked if I would like to see other areas of interest in the Medellín metropolitan community. I told him I was actually quite tired and wanted to go and meditate. We parted ways and he called a cab to take me back up to the compound. I spent the rest of the afternoon talking with Vicki and swimming in the beautiful pool which had been cleaned and filled with water.

Father Gabriel arrived back at the compound for dinner and prepared a meal of rice, beans, and chicken with fresh fruit for the both of us. We again started telling stories and enjoying each other's company. After several stories, we retired to our rooms for rest and sleep.

Chapter 20 - Sunday, A Day of Rest?

June 7, 2015

I awoke early today with desires for meditation and prayer. I started out with my mantra, ascending quickly into the other realms of consciousness. Archangel Gabriel, the Archangel of messages, appeared to me. He told me I was on my path, which was to become an author and speaker to the masses. He told me I needed to be on a spiritual path and that my family and I would be protected and taken care of.

Archangel Gabriel also said that I would need to complete the book about Father Gabriel and then create a St. Germaine sanctuary in St. George, Utah. He stated I would be traveling and teaching about the 24-strand DNA manifestation and helping people prepare mentally, spiritually and physically for the ascension. He then reiterated the importance of staying on a spiritual path and that I would be blessed with health, strength, and a long life. I immediately came out of the meditation and vision with an attitude of gratitude and knowing I was on my path.

Father Gabriel found it very important to give people holidays and rest. Maria had another day off, so he was busy making breakfast for the four of us. We sat down and ate wonderful food with the love of Father Gabriel cooked right into it. When we finished, Fathers José and Orlando went off to different parishes, to give the gift of the Mass in other locations.

After cleaning up the kitchen and the dishes, Father Gabriel and I walked down the path to the larger building down by the swimming pool. We entered the conference center at 9:30 AM. Father Gabriel put on a white priestly robe and prepared for celebration of the Missa, or Mass.

This was the first time I experienced Father Gabriel performing ritual for the Catholic Church. As he proceeded, I could feel his dedication to help the people grow spiritually as well as mentally and physically. Several unfamiliar faces of local people appeared and sat down in the chairs provided to celebrate the Mass with Father Gabriel. We partook of the body and blood of Christ with a beautiful contemplation of the last supper. Everyone participating could feel the Love of Christ present in the room.

Father Gabriel spent the next hour after Mass talking with all the people who came. The energy of love and acceptance was so strong in the room that everyone shed tears of joy and peace.

Once everyone had gone, Father Gabriel asked, "Where would Dr. Scott like to eat lunch?" I answered, "I'm here with you so I would like to go wherever you go after Mass." As he removed his robes he stated, "Let's go down to the mall. I will take you to my favorite spot."

We got into the white Volkswagen and it was the first time I experienced Father Gabriel driving. Instead of going left to the main road down the hill, we took a right, which took us over to the local mall. It was a large building with many stores, very similar to malls in the United States. The only difference was the many tropical trees within the mall. There were also many more walkways with beautiful views of the city down below. We sat down in a restaurant which was open to the air, but had a glass covering above us to keep rain off the visitors. This was Father Gabriel's favorite restaurant and I told him to order me what he was going to have.

The food was brought out to us along with two Colombian coffees, made the way Father Gabriel loved, which was delicious. Fresh tropical fruit adorned the meal and the Colombian fried chicken was seasoned to perfection. Father Gabriel used his utensils to begin with, then grabbed the chicken with his fingers, so I too could eat with my fingers.

When we finished our lunch, Father Gabriel wanted to walk around the mall. This level of the mall was circular and we walked six times through the hallways around very beautifully designed department stores and smaller shops. The entire floor represented shops found in America. Father Gabriel was glad that he had me as a companion to walk and talk with, as he usually spent Sundays alone.

He then asked, "Do you mind if we do the shopping for the week?" I answered, "I'm here to be with you and get to know you better."

We walked down to the parking garage, got back into the white Volkswagen and drove down several streets to a big white building that looked like a Costco warehouse. It was named differently, but as we walked in everything was familiar, including the foods, some Kirkland brands and even the location of all the familiar products. It was a Colombian Costco store. Father Gabriel filled his cart with organic food, Colombian coffee, and a variety of treats he always had on hand for the children.

We checked out and headed to the parking garage where we put all the groceries into the car. The groceries had been boxed up so they were easily transferred into the car. Father Gabriel drove us back up to the compound where we gave the boxes to two men who were waiting for us.

Father Gabriel then took me for a tour of the area surrounding the compound. He asked if I had questions and I asked as many as I could. It was a very pleasant afternoon discussing many topics in a beautiful environment.

Father Gabriel is a dedicated, congenial, kind and educated

human being. His only desire is to serve the people, inspire them, teach them, and help them access their higher self through meditation and transformation. He has studied psychology, sociology, higher ministry and parochial education. He has associated himself with the higher ministries of the Catholic Church and yet he desired to return to Colombia to help the people he loves so much.

He discussed all the locations of Hogares Claret throughout South America and how several over the last 10 years have been opened up in Central America and Mexico. He has filled all the leadership positions with previous students who have been educated and have served in the Hogares Claret, so now he has a self-propagating system of rehabilitation and education. He stated that he wants to continue to serve, love, and inspire each location for the rest of his life.

Father Gabriel was able to visit each location every month until there became so many, and now he's lucky to visit each one every four months. His aspiration is to continue to grow and expand Hogares Claret throughout all the Americas. As he spoke about this, I told him we need his homes in the United States, as our success rate of rehabilitation treatment is dismal compared to his Hogares Claret. He smiled and stated, "When they are ready, and maybe your book will help them get ready."

Father Gabriel, the other Fathers, and the many dedicated workers created a beautiful organization to help all these children and young adults, bringing them into a productive adulthood. The outcome of this program is highly successful. Ninety-eight percent of the children and young adults that enter the program and complete all the requirements, education and meditation programs return to society as highly evolved human beings, substance and addiction free. Each of them have a new life purpose and know their existence matters. They have the tools to be successful and the desire to make the world a better place.

Padre Gabriel, through all his education and service, is helping all of South and Central America through the programs of the Hogares Claret, integrating the "disposable ones" back into society with more resilience and integrity, healthier backgrounds and habits. All of the adults I met who had graduated from the program were well educated, well dressed, interacted with others in integrity and intelligence. With Transcendental Meditation as a basis for their soul, they felt like they were all integrated higher beings of light. Because of all of their histories, they showed compassion and love and seemed to have a higher purpose and view of life. They were nonjudgmental because they had been in life situations and places of being judged.

Each individual coming out of Hogares Claret was grounded to the earth, physically conscious, environmentally connected to the earth, but also connected to the heavens.

The education system within the Hogares Claret surpassed my expectations, as many of the teachers themselves had been past students of the homes. They knew of the difficulties each child faced living in the streets, as they had been there themselves. They were very helpful in changing attitudes and understanding the past experiences of all the children.

Padre Gabriel and the other Fathers had taken all of the best systems of psychology, nutrition, re-education and reintegration and joined them together to create homes for the children and young adults with a family atmosphere. These children had been thrown away by society and drug wars, many with parents who were dead, creating an environment of mental, emotional, physical and spiritual damage. Father Gabriel had created a healing environment, retraining thousands of children and young adults with a success rate far surpassing anything I had seen in the entire world.

The following is a list of some of the additional accomplishments of Padre Gabriel:

1961 Father Gabriel Graduated from the Claretian Seminary in Bogotá, Colombia

1975 Father Gabriel met Maharishi

1982 Father Gabriel learned to meditate

1983 Father Gabriel decided to come back to Colombia to repair damage done to his people in the country of Colombia

1983 Father Gabriel opened the first Hogares Claret in Medellín, Colombia

1986 Depok Chopra taught Father Gabriel Transcendental Meditation

1987 Father Gabriel attended an International Psychiatric Association conference in Vienna, Austria, where Logotherapy was taught and accepted. It was part of the psychotherapeutic school of thought founded by Viktor Frankl, often called the "Third Viennese Psychiatric School of Thought" (after Freud's Psychoanalysis and Adler's and Jung's Individual Psychotherapy).

1987 Santa Elena facility was bought from The South American meditation organization which had started through the work of Maharishi Mahesh Yogananda in 1975

1987 Maharishi Center of Academia Professors of Latin America was sold to Hogares Claret

1988 Father Gabriel taught his family members who desired to learn Transcendental Meditation

1989 Father Gabriel initiated the Siddhis, progressing in his meditation practice

Quotation of Father Gabriel: "Drop by drop, breaks hard rocks."

1989 Hogares Claret of Mira Flores opened up for the children

Chapter 21 - Boy Scout Camp

June 8, 2015

Three Boy Scouts appeared early this morning while I was out on the porch meditating. They asked where Father Gabriel was, so I answered, "I believe he is in the kitchen." They headed straight to the kitchen and asked if they could eat and visit with Padre Gabriel, who greeted them excitedly. "But of course," he said in a kindly manner.

Padre Gabriel is always happy, delighted, and conversant with everyone who comes into his life. The boys were part of the camping retreat of the Boy Scouts of Colombia at the compound, staying down in the apartment-like structure by the swimming pool. They were all curious about who I was and what I was doing there.

Father Gabriel introduced me and told them I was an American doctor interested in the work of the Three Fathers. He said I was writing a book about all the Hogares Claret and the success they were having with the children and adults. Each boy was very curious and started asking me questions about my life, what it was like to be a doctor in the United States, and what had led me to Colombia to be with, and learn from Father Gabriel.

I told them, "I am extremely grateful to be led to Father Gabriel and St. Germaine, who is an ascended Master like Jesus, was actually the one guiding me to him. I voluntarily relinquished practicing medicine in the United States, because I believed natural herbs, homeopathic remedies, flower essences and essential oils were much better and caused fewer side effects for healing. Padre Gabriel also uses all these modalities to help in the healing of the humans in his care."

These Boy Scouts were all very happy and excited that I was writing a book about Father Gabriel.

After quickly inhaling their breakfast, they thanked Father Gabriel and ran off down the hill to participate in all the activities of their Scout troop.

I finished my breakfast as well, then we headed back up the mountain to Hogares Claret in Santa Elena, where Camilo Estrada also works as an Ayurvedic pulse reader. Practitioners of Ayurveda medicine gather much physical information from the radial pulse in the wrist, tuning into the body with intuition. Camilo also cleans the people with Panchakarma (five actions) or PK, which is a cleansing and rejuvenating program for the body, mind and consciousness. It is known for its beneficial effects on overall health, wellness and self-healing. According to Ayurveda, our natural state is one of health, happiness, and an inner sense of well-being. Health is defined as the body being clear of toxins, the mind being at peace, and emotions being calm and happy. Waste products are efficiently eliminated from the body and the organs are functioning normally.

In our busy, stressful and toxic world, our physical, emotional, and mental systems accumulate stress and toxins causing sickness, addictions, and disease. This eventually weakens our organs, nerves, and vital systems, opening the door for chronic, degenerative, and inflammatory diseases to develop. Panchakarma can help reverse these negative effects of daily living.

The therapy involves using cleansing herbs internally, essential oil massage with cleansing and calming oils, and pouring therapeutic oils on the head, soothing and washing away the emotions and mental stress. Lifestyle and dietary recommendations are taught, specific to each individual. These include healing herbal teas, light healing nutrition, vegetarian foods and a supportive environment that provides space for true contemplation and continued self-healing. Herbal Rasayanas (rejuvenatives) are also provided to take after completion of the program. Meditation is taught to calm the emotions and center the individual. Opportunity for all these healing modalities, as well as Panchakarma therapy, is available for residents and visitors coming to Hogares Claret at Santa Elena.

Padre Gabriel had an important meeting to attend, so Camilo spoke with me for a short time, then his assistant took me outside again to the therapy horses and past the large garden of "birds of paradise" flowers.

The air was fresh and delightful after the rainstorm the night before and my shoes had mud all over them. We walked for about 30 minutes on the land Padre Gabriel had obtained from Maharishi many years ago, where the priests had lived and worked with the teachers of Transcendental Meditation for several years.

In 2002, with the help of Alan from Belgium, Father Gabriel Mejia bought the property from the International Society of Meditation and prepared the property to be used as Hogares Claret. There is also a primary and secondary school being constructed near the Hogares Claret in Santa Elena and Padre Gabriel donated the land to the local government for the school to be built. It will be for the entire community and also for children of the workers at Hogares Claret in Santa Elena.

Father Gabriel has a plan and a good heart full of love. As I followed him, I could see him contemplating all the land and buildings around the grounds, imagining how to create better facilities, better environments, and happier circumstances for every person he meets.

When we were finished with our day, we said our goodbyes with hugs and loving messages, loaded up into the 15 passenger van and headed back down the mountain.

When we arrived at the central offices, Father José and Father Orlando were waiting for us. Father Gabriel climbed the stairs and headed down to his office, collecting some more material to work on at the house compound.

It was raining and traffic was much worse than usual for our trip home. As I looked out the window, I saw several children selling flowers in the street and for the first time I asked the Fathers to stop so I could buy some flowers from them. Father Gabriel was pleased. When we arrived at the compound, I asked Maria for a vase and she put the flowers in the living room. Dinner was ready so we headed into the dining room for another feast with fresh tropical fruit, chicken and rice, and another delicious dessert. Afterward, Father Gabriel turned on his favorite news channel from Germany, which we watched for about an hour, said our departing good nights, and retired to our rooms.

Chapter 22 - A Day of Healing

June 9, 2015

I awoke to the pitter patter of rain on the roof. I wondered if the scouts were all warm in their beds or if they had slept outside in tents. Since it was only 3 AM, I decided I would meditate. Thoughts of Father Gabriel came into my mind, thoughts of his kindness and love for all the children and people in the world and the organization.

As I said my mantra I ascended, finding myself in the center of the universe. Then I had thoughts of the hierarchy of the universe, the great central sun and the seven Elohim and rays of light coming out of the void, creating all the stars, planets, moons, and heavens, creating worlds without measure, home for all of nature and the elements.

I fell back to sleep while the rain continued dancing on the roof. The next sound I heard was Father Gabriel celebrating mass, so it must've been 5:00 AM. I decided to get up and start my day.

I grabbed my razor and started my morning ritual of shaving and then showering, first turning on the water, getting wet, turning off the water, washing my hair and then soaping up. I would then turn on the water and rinse off all the soap. The water would be on for 15 seconds while I was getting wet. It would take about 60 seconds of the water being on to rinse. This had been my method of showering since I had been on a service mission in Puerto Rico, learning how to conserve water.

I unlocked the front door and walked out on the porch as the sun was rising in the east. It was time to Facetime Vicki. We had a wonderful conversation for over an hour and a half talking about all the things that had happened the previous day with our children and our experiences.

Father Gabriel soon called out, "Dr. Scott, breakfast is served." I said my goodbyes to Vicki and headed quickly into the dining room to a breakfast with mango, pineapple, and papaya. Fathers José and Orlando had returned in the night and greeted me as I entered the dining room.

I asked Maria, "Is passion fruit available?" She stated, "Yes we have it, and I will go cut it up for you." Maria went into the kitchen, peeled and sliced the passion fruit into beautiful slices and brought it out on a plate.

"Thank you Maria, you are so kind." I said. The passion fruit was sweet, delicious and very juicy. I wanted to take good care of my pancreas, and this trip to Colombia had been so pleasant and happy that my pancreas was very content.

We finished our breakfast, packed up our cases and headed down the steps of the path to the white Volkswagen. Father José was again driving, Father Orlando was next to me in the back seat and Father Gabriel was in front of me. He questioned me, "I would like you to think about what you would like to do these final two days in Colombia. You will have time today at the office to decide, as I have much to do in the main offices today." Father Gabriel was always considerate of other people's time and efforts. By this time, he knew I flew by the seat of my pants in making decisions. We discussed earlier at breakfast that I received a call from Monica Tovar, who wanted me to come to Bucaramanga, Colombia. During my meditation, the spirit said that I should spend another two days with Father Gabriel, then fly out early Thursday morning to Bucaramanga. Father Gabriel was saddened with this news, but also wanted me to follow spirit.

We traveled down the mountain easily with Father José driving to the central offices of Hogares Claret, where we were again greeted by all the employees. Father Gabriel had meetings all morning and announced he was going to see his alternative medical doctor for an appointment in the afternoon. He asked, "Would you like to join me?" to which I answered, "For sure."

I sat on the nice brown couch in Father Gabriel's office, writing down the many activities of the past few days on my iPad mini. Around 11:30 AM, one of the female employees came up and asked me if I would like some lunch. I followed her down to the pool area, which had a covered dining area with three long tables big enough for 24 people to sit around.

A lunch of rice soup, chicken and white rice with fruit and dessert was served, which I quickly gobbled up. I've been told many times that I eat my food too quickly, that I should sit and savor, enjoying the food and chewing better. Since Father Gabriel was to be in meetings for at least another hour, I decided to walk out in the streets of Medellín for 40 minutes.

I asked the secretary to unlock the front door and said, "I will be back in 40 minutes. I will stay close by and just get some fresh air." She questioned, "Do you need someone to go with you?" I felt very comfortable walking on my own so I replied, "No thank you," as I headed out of the front door of Hogares Claret, crossed the street at the stop light, and walked three blocks to the south. There were many shops and little stores along the way. An espresso shop caught my attention since I was feeling tired after eating lunch. I walked in and ordered café Americana which was the closest thing to what I was used to in the United States. The cost was minimal, about $.40 in American dollars. The flavor was wonderful and they had added whipped cream on top which made it even better. Since it was in a "to go" cup, I headed out back down the street, looking in all the various shops with curiosity.

I found the Colombians to be a very happy and open people. As I walked down the street, they all could tell I was from the United States and would try to talk to me in English. I would always answer them in Spanish, which actually impressed them and put a smile upon their faces. Many asked what I was doing there in Colombia, if I was with the CIA. I would explain to them that I was an author writing a book about Father Gabriel and Hogares Claret. Some of the people of the street had heard about him and the organization of Hogares Claret, but I was surprised how many hadn't heard about him or Hogares Claret. Only about half the people I talked to knew anything of his programs or homes for the street children. Some, in fact, thought Hogares Claret was a program of the government and not of a private organization.

I instructed these people, twelve of them having gathered around me listening, of Father Gabriel and Hogares Claret as best I could, and all of them were very grateful. They would say, "A Catholic priest is taking care of the street children." I would say to them, "Yes, and he's having a 98% success rate rehabilitating the children," to which they would reply, "That's amazing, that's wonderful, how do we learn more about this?" I stated, "Their headquarters is just two blocks away and they have pamphlets, DVDs and information."

All the people I met and talked to about this seemed very happy and grateful to know someone was attending to these children. I headed back to the headquarters to find Father Gabriel worried about me. "Where have you been, Dr. Scott? I'm ready to go to my appointment." "I'm sorry, Father Gabriel, but I went for a walk, and gave a little lecture about you and Hogares Claret and lost track of the time." The secretary at the front desk had told Father Gabriel I had gone for a walk and told her I would be right back. I was gone for a full hour.

Father Gabriel and I entered the white Volkswagen, backed out of the garage into the busy street and were on our way. We traveled to a very nice part of Medellín with new shops, new houses with trees, shrubbery, and yards full of green tropical plants and flowers. We pulled up to a professionally constructed business building with a man standing in a parking place. The man guided Father Gabriel, who quickly pulled into the parking space. The man opened the driver's door, greeting Father Gabriel and telling him, "It is such a pleasure to see you." Father Gabriel responded in kind. The man took Father Gabriel's hand, helping him out of the car, and they hugged. You could tell they had known each other for a long time.

We entered the building which had several suites with doctors' names on the doors. The receptionist quickly took us to a room with an examination table. Father Gabriel explained about several of the instruments in the room and how the doctor would use these to assist with patients' healing. I recognized some of the instruments and devices as alternative healing devices used in the United States. Some of them were unfamiliar.

The doctor, a middle-aged woman in a white laboratory coat, entered with a wide grin, saying, "Good afternoon, Father Gabriel, how are you feeling today?" Father Gabriel stated, "I'm doing much better, but I still have pain in my head (pointing at his third eye), and in my mouth and neck."

She quickly energetically scanned Father Gabriel's body, a talent few medical doctors know about. She took out a crystal along with another device I was unfamiliar with and started to describe how these devices would help move the energy to a proper alignment with his meridians. She stated, "Some of the meridians of the neck, shoulders, and head are not flowing properly." I reassuringly said, "I am very familiar with alternative and energy medicine." She smiled and nodded, as her hands continued her treatment.

I asked, "Where did you do your training?" She stated, "I attended medical school and trained in Spain and also trained in alternative and energy medicine in Europe." She placed another device on Father Gabriel's shoulders and back, and described how this device would help repair his emotions in his liver, pancreas, and spleen.

During the treatment, Father Gabriel was very open and receptive to the healing. I felt like I was with my own people and was very impressed with this Colombian medical doctor's knowledge and treatments. We were there for about 45 minutes, the doctor and Father Gabriel conversing like they were old friends. In fact, I found out they had known each other for many years and Father Gabriel had brought children in for treatment also.

When the treatments were done, Father Gabriel and the medical doctor said their goodbyes with hugs and handshakes. The man who had parked us was still standing by the white Volkswagen. He opened the door for Father Gabriel as he got in, and then Father Gabriel started the car and we were on our way back to the compound in the mountains of Enviago.

When we returned to the house overlooking the compound, we entered and put our bags down and went into the dining room where dinner was being served. Father José and Father Orlando were already seated, sipping some delightful juice that Maria had prepared. They invited Father Gabriel and myself to taste the delicious brew. Maria had remembered that I enjoyed pineapple, passion fruit and papaya and she had made a smoothie of these three delicious tropical fruits. As she brought the dinner meal in, I said, "I am so grateful to you, Maria, for providing us with such delicious food and for going out of your way to produce this juice." She answered, "It is a pleasure to serve you."

I asked Father Gabriel, "Are you pleased with your accomplishments in this life?"

Father Gabriel answered, "I have had a very fortunate life, being guided from the beginning with my birth into a beautiful family, with spiritual parents who taught me about Jesus and about spirituality and compassion. My mother and father were servants to all the people, giving freely of their time, money and fortune. We were taught to do the same."

Father Gabriel continued, "I dedicated my life to God in the service of his people. I have never regretted any moment of my life or decisions. I live my life for the children and for creating an environment for healing and growth. I continuously send the energy of love, bombs of love, to all the children on the planet Earth."

I asked Father Gabriel, "What are your plans for the future?" Father Gabriel answered, "To continue to serve all the children in the streets. To continue opening more safe Hogares Claret in South and Central America, Mexico and possibly, the Caribbean." I thanked him for his answers and for allowing me to come and stay at his house. Father Gabriel said, "This house is not mine, it is a house dedicated to God, and He has allowed all of us to be here." Fathers José and Orlando agreed.

Father José retrieved an atlas from their library and wanted me to point out where St. George, Utah was on the map. I described that we lived in a most beautiful desert on the earth. Four national parks were within less than two hours drive – Zion National Park, the North Rim of the Grand Canyon, Cedar Breaks and Bryce Canyon National Park.

He then asked about my family, and I told him, "I started out my life in circumstances that were not optimal. My birth father and mother divorced before I was one year old. My mother supported three children by being a secretary for the Department of Highways for the State of Utah. Luckily, my grandparents lived nearby and helped to raise me. My grandfather was a Mormon bishop for 25 years, a man very dedicated to God and the people in the community. My grandmother was a happy, wonderful, caring person. They taught me and helped me for the first 10 years of my life.

"My mother remarried, to a construction engineer, who changed all of our lives by moving us to southern Utah. He had money and lived his life and taught us about abundance. We never lacked for anything. We would get out into nature every weekend, go on family vacations, and lived a life that many envied. He was a good Catholic, but seldom attended church. My mother was a Mormon, but seldom attended church. Church was out in nature as I grew up. I thrived in this environment, did very well in school, attended the University in Cedar City, Utah, graduating with very high honors. I married, had two baby boys, and worked very hard prior to being accepted to a Jesuit medical school in St. Louis, Missouri. I graduated from St. Louis University Medical School on May 18, 1986. On May 20, 1986, a baby girl was added to my family.

"During medical school I had moonlighted working for a company of lawyers called Colburn Krofts and Putszel. There, I was in charge of going through medical charts of linemen for the telephone and electrical companies, correlating their exposure to agent orange and dioxin to their symptoms and diseases relating to this exposure. We found there was a correlation and the lawsuit of the some 8000 men ended up being settled out of court and the information buried by the judge. This job had made me very aware of the impact of chemicals on our environment and our bodies.

"During my internship in St. Louis University Hospitals, I was on call one night and was contacted by a frantic nurse regarding a woman with stage IV vaginal cancer. I had assisted the attending physician to place tubes filled with radioactive iridium to kill the diseased tissues in her pelvis. The caps on the tubes had not been adequately sealed and tightened, and the radioactive iridium was burning the buttocks and thighs of the woman, causing her to scream out in constant pain. I approached the room, with signs out front of the door stating, 'Highly radioactive, do not enter.'

"I was the only one available in the middle of the night to assist this woman. I made the decision to enter the room, putting on a leaded apron, leaded gloves, leaded helmet and mask, protecting myself as best I could. I examined the tubes leaking radioactive material with her in a supine position and I told her I was there to help. I replaced and tightened the seals on the tubes. I cleaned the material underneath her and placed it in a radioactive containment bin. I then carried her and washed her burnt skin carefully and applied Silvadene to the burns. This woman had thought she was going to be left to die alone. She said to me, 'You are my saving Angel,' several times. I placed her back into the cleaned bed and placed a warm blanket over her chilled body. I put all the contaminated material safely away and left the leaded apron, gloves, and mask in a container by the door.

"The next morning during rounds, the attending surgical physician told me how stupid I was, entering the room and assisting this woman who was going to die from her cancer anyway. He said, 'I want you off from my service.' He then asked to see my radiation badge and in horror saw that it had gone black. He again muttered about my stupidity, how I had exposed myself to a lethal dose of radiation. I still believe I did the right thing with the radiation leakage. I knew I was not going to die, but I also knew I didn't have the answers.

"I transferred to Phoenix, Arizona, within the next two months to complete my residency in obstetrics and gynecology. Within a year of the exposure to the radiation, I developed stage IV invasive malignant melanoma resistant to chemotherapy and radiation. I had several tumors on my spine and brain and the primary tumor on the skin on my right shoulder of my back with a small thread of tumors traveling deep into my spine. I was told there was nothing medically or surgically to be done and that I would probably be dead within 2 to 3 months. I knew I wasn't going to die. I went home that night with a prayer in my heart knowing I would have an answer.

"During the night, I kept hearing the name, 'Hulda Clark.' I awoke early the next morning wondering who this person was. When I arrived at work and went to my desk, which was usually laden with many charts needing signatures and revisions, the desk had been cleared off, with only an article in the center of the desk, by a Dr. Hulda Clark, a microbiologist out of Chicago Illinois. The scientific article was about how parasites, fungi, viruses and toxins cause cancer and by removing these components the cancer could be cured. Dr. Clark's address and telephone number were on the last page of the article. I hurriedly dialed the number and to my surprise Dr. Clark answered the phone. For the next two hours, I talked with her about my condition and story. She told me the treatments I needed to do to cure my condition. I did exactly what she told me, using chelation, parasite cleansing, herbal anti-fungals, herbal antivirals, Essiac tea and cat's claw, and within two months all the tumors were gone. Dr. Clark had told me to continue the treatment for two years and then to continue taking parasite cleansers for two weeks every quarter. "

I discussed with the Three Fathers several other stories which had brought me to Colombia. They were all delighted to hear my stories of faith, healing, and divine direction. We all hugged, said our good nights, and went to bed with our faith increased and joy in our hearts.

Chapter 23 - My Last Day with Father Gabriel

June 10, 2015

Again, I awoke to the pitter patter of the rain. It always delighted me, coming from a desert in southern Utah, so I thanked the water and air fairies in Colombia for bringing the rain every morning.

I started meditating, saying my mantra, transcending deeply into the universe to a planet called Arcturus, a very old planet with extremely evolved humanoids. It is a beautiful planet, with seven large, bright silver, shiny cities suspended in the blue atmosphere. A beautiful golden white shining being of light approached me saying, "Behold, my loved one, I am Arcturus, one of the seven mighty Elohim, and I have come to you with a message. We have entered a time or dispensation of the culmination of 26,000 years of evolution of this work on the planet Earth. This new generation currently incarnating on your earth will lead the ascension of all humans ready to move into the higher octaves of creation. This generation is being led by the seven Elohim, seven Archangels, the sacred light of the seven Rays and the seven directors of the seven Rays of light.

"You will be asked to create sanctuaries of light, teaching, declaring, meditating, and praying, for the enlightenment and evolution for the ascension in North America, Central America and South America," declared Arcturus. "From the Americas, the teachings will spread to the entire world."

Arcturus then placed his hands of light upon my head, declaring, "As you leave Father Gabriel, Bless him as I Am Blessing you now. I

Bless you Scott, with the Three-fold Flame of Divine Love, Wisdom, and Power, and the Unfed Flame of creation, to be placed over and protecting the Third Eye of Creative Visualization, to protect all you Project and Manifest in Righteousness. This will Protect your work and the work of the 'I Am Presence' to Be At-One-Ment. Then go forth, and give the Blessings of Heaven to all those you meet who desire healing and evolution. With each blessing, I will Protect and seal your and their auric fields, to receive these Blessings, in the name of the Father, and of the Son and of the Holy Spirit. So be it and so it is, I Am that I Am."

Arcturus then left me, more enlightened and in peace.

The sounds of the Fathers penetrated my room as they celebrated the Mass. It was actually a very pleasant way to wake each morning and I was at the end of my sabbatical. I got up and showered, shaved my face, then made my way to the front door, unlocked it, and stepped outside to a beautiful morning. Each morning I would Facetime Vicki and report on the progress of each day. I told her about the dream of Arcturus and it was received with loving and supportive remarks.

At breakfast Father Gabriel asked what my itinerary was for the flight to Bucaramanga. The flight was leaving at 5 AM so he suggested I get up at 3:30 AM and said his driver would pick me up at that time and take me to the airport in Rio Negro. He stated he had many business meetings today and that I was welcome to join him or go to another Hogares Claret. The nearest one to where we were was an hour and a half away, which was too far since it meant a three-hour drive. I told him I would rather remain around him and go with him to his meetings if I could. He was agreeable to that and so our date was set with me being able to listen and learn from Father Gabriel.

After breakfast we brushed our teeth and headed down the familiar path, past the archery range to the white Volkswagen. The

30-minute drive down the mountain to the valley below was getting very familiar. I was beginning to know the streets and their names and we passed familiar faces on the way to the main offices. We pulled into the garage and entered through the door to be greeted with smiling faces and hugs as we started another day.

The first meeting was up in the boardroom; about 12 people had gathered already when we walked in and Father Gabriel introduced me again with his special voice saying, "I would like to introduce Dr. Scott. For those of you who have not met him, he is from the state of Utah in the United States of America." I recognized three faces, and the others were from other areas in Colombia who had come to meet with Father Gabriel. This meeting was deciding about expanding into Central America and Venezuela. New directors were being selected and plans were being made to expand Hogares Claret.

The conversation was very businesslike, but also very spiritual in that each man held a love in his heart for Father Gabriel and the programs. They discussed projected enrollment and properties which would fulfill the requirements of the children and their housing, cafeteria, instructional facilities, and areas for play. They had already brought illustrations and diagrams of facilities available for purchase and the negotiated buying price. It was like watching a well-oiled machine as these beautiful men continued with their life's work.

The meeting lasted until lunch time, concluded, and we all headed down to the pool and kitchen area with tables. The entire group sat down and asked me to give the blessing on the food. As I had served a mission in Spanish, I easily blessed the food and blessed all those present as Arcturus had asked me to do. Father Gabriel smiled reassuringly and thanked me for the blessings. I knew I was to continue to do this during the rest of my stay in Colombia. After lunch, Father Gabriel gave hugs and handshakes to all those present and added his blessings for Godspeed in their duties.

In the afternoon, there was another meeting in the boardroom with a different set of individuals, also discussing the opening of several other various Hogares Claret in Brazil and another in Colombia. I didn't recognize the names of the cities, but my soul was soaring, knowing Father Gabriel was creating more Hogares Claret for the children and for the people in Central and South America. Father Gabriel was extremely aware of the importance of families in the rehabilitation process. They were always invited and included in all the activities if they were available. The meetings continued till 4 PM, at which time final comments and resolutions were made and the plans finalized. Everyone participating in the meetings felt the seriousness of the process, and the meetings were very productive.

Father Gabriel made us both a cup of Colombian coffee, with sugar and cream, down in his office. He then excused himself to give his goodbyes to the men from the meeting. He returned in about half an hour, telling me he needed to go through the paperwork and then we would head back to the compound of the Three Fathers.

I could tell on the ride home that Father Gabriel was quite deep in thought, and then he asked the question, "Did you get all the information, Dr. Scott?" I answered him, "I have had a wonderful time learning from you, the other Fathers, and all the employees of Hogares Claret. I have so much information about your success and programs. I want to be able to put it together in a logical, yet readable fashion. My desire is also to tell the wonderful healing occurring with all these children." Father Gabriel smiled.

We arrived at the compound with a honk and the large metal door slid open. We pulled past the swimming pool into the parking place next to the large building where Boy Scouts still gathered in groups working for merit badges. Several of the scouts were using bows and arrows on the archery range, shooting their arrows at targets, getting their archery merit badges. Father Gabriel spent time greeting each scout, somehow knowing each by name and something about their families, as we slowly made our way up the path. I could tell he knew each boy, even though he met hundreds every week. He truly took an interest in each individual and their progress and he knew about them and loved them.

That night at the dinner table, the Three Fathers and I had a wonderful discussion. Each one of them had many questions about me from the night before. They were interested in learning more. They were especially interested in hearing about stories of miracle healing, so I told about when, five years previously, Vicki and I woke up with the feeling we were supposed to move to North Carolina. So we put up the house for sale, scheduled a flight to Charlotte, North Carolina, and made arrangements with a local herb store, so that I could do intuitive readings to help defray the costs for the flights and hotels. We had made arrangements with the real estate late agent to show us homes in our price range. It was post-2008, after the mortgage industry had collapsed, and a $500,000 house was selling for about $200,000. Vicki and I smiled at each other as we viewed the beautiful homes where we could raise our family.

In the afternoon, we headed to the herb store in the older part of Charlotte. In those days, I would quickly look at a person's aura, determine what would help them and pick out products in the herb store to assist the owners in their sales. It would take anywhere from 10 to 15 minutes including dosages. I had done seven of these readings, when a young black woman came in with a little girl. The woman was dragging her right leg, her right arm hung from her shoulder and her face was gaunt and paralyzed on the right side. She pronounced, "I have been praying for months to be healed, and you came. I know that you can heal me." At first my thoughts were, "Who am I to heal you?" Then I heard in my mind, "Three," and heard her guides tell me she had a stroke at the age of three years old. Taking courage, I said to this young woman, "You had a stroke at the age of three years old." She answered, "I had three strokes when I was three years old, from sickle cell anemia, which left my entire right side paralyzed. I know you have come to heal me." I stated, "I will do my best."

I had recently learned the technique of visualization, visualizing energy tubules, re-organizing nerves, muscles, tendons, and ligaments, to be placed in perfection within the body. I closed my eyes, called upon all energy tubules to come back to the individual through space, time, and dimension, reintegrating in perfection in the body, in this case on this beautiful young woman's right side. I could hear sounds of amazement coming from the people in the room, so I opened my eyes and to my astonishment this young woman was straightening up and moving her right arm and leg, her face became more normal in appearance and she spoke very clearly, "Thank you for blessing and healing me." She left without her cane, holding her daughter's left hand with her right hand. I was so dumbfounded that I had to take a break from the readings.

I saw 60 other people over the next couple days and each one received knowledge and blessings, with an herbal regimen. But I could not get that young woman out of my mind. It was a miracle.

We spent the next morning looking at beautiful homes, and decided to attend the Unity Church of Charlotte at 11 AM. We picked the church randomly from the computer and it felt intuitively, that is where we were supposed to go. We arrived at the church and the pastor, a woman, met us at the door and welcomed us to the morning services. As we entered, we noticed a black woman in a wheelchair on the back row, wearing flip flops. She had smelly feet, and both feet appeared to have gangrene. As I was checking out her feet she looked at me with the brown eyes of a woman with questions.

Vicki picked a spot with two chairs close to the front of the chapel. The pastor started telling the story of how the Unity Church started. It began on the frontier with a married couple with health problems. The woman had a disease called consumption, which is called tuberculosis in our modern terms. It was slowly killing her, consuming her body. The husband had been run over by a wagon at a young age and had lost the use of his right hip. He had to use a cane to get around. Someone had told this young woman that if she would place a chair in front of her, and put another chair where she would sit and visualize Jesus in the chair in front of her, healing her, she would be healed. So this young woman would sit in a chair facing an empty chair every day for an hour, for over a month. The tuberculosis left her body and she became well, able to do her chores and even help her husband in the fields.

Her husband asked her, "Do you think I can be healed if I do the same thing that you have done?" She answered him, "You need to have faith, and I believe you can be healed." The husband was a nonbeliever, had never believed in Jesus and in fact, cursed Jesus for his disability. The wife knowing this, told him, "You don't have to believe; sitting there visualizing Jesus healing you will be enough faith for you to heal."

So the husband started out first making it a few days, and then a few weeks, and then a few months. He persisted and his faith grew, and his visualization efforts grew. Then one morning as he sat in the chair visualizing Jesus healing him, he felt a pop in his hip as the head of his femur bone popped back into place. He quickly stood, giving out praises to Jesus, and ran out of the house to find his healed wife working in the field. The story of this miraculous couple spread far and wide and their method of healing started up in many prairie homes.

The pastor then stood and asked, looking at Vicki and me, "Would you like to introduce yourselves to the congregation?" Vicki stood up and moved to the front pulpit. She stated that we were moving to North Carolina and that we were very grateful to the local church. She introduced me, and the congregation was very interested to hear us both speak. I was told to do a breathing technique and to teach it to them. I did the breathing technique involving all the nerve centers and the associated glands, with each of the seven chakras. When it was completed the congregation seemed very pleased. The pastor then gave closing remarks and prayed, blessing everyone in the congregation with healing.

The pastor then joined Vicki and me, walking us toward the door and asked, "Would you both like to eat lunch with the congregation?" Before I could answer, the black woman with the gangrenous feet who had been sitting at the back in the wheelchair pulled me to the side. "You came to heal me," she said emphatically. I quickly scanned her body and felt she had diabetes, with extremely high sugars which had damaged the nerves in her legs and feet causing diabetic ulcers and ultimately the gangrene in her feet. She could tell I was scanning her, and again stated, "I know you can heal me, I've been praying for months not to lose my feet, and I am scheduled for surgery tomorrow to have them removed. Jesus told me you would be at my church today and that you would heal me." As I looked at her gangrenous feet my courage left me and faith was not in my mind. Then, I thought about the healing of the 28-year-old mother who had been healed the day before, and I began to take courage because of the miracle which had taken place. Then I thought, "I can use the same technique, and by using that technique I can have the faith to help her heal." So I asked her, "Do you have the faith to heal?" She answered quickly, "I know I can heal and I know you came to help me." So I started visualizing the energy tubules, gathering them from space, time, and dimension, directing them to perfected fields of energy in her feet. I visualized the subcutaneous tissues perfected and healed. I could hear sounds of amazement from the people surrounding us, and I opened my eyes to see perfected feet at the bottom of her legs. The gangrene was gone, as was the smell, and a fragrance of roses entered into my nostrils. I knew the Angel of the Roses was there with us assisting with the healing energy of Jesus. She stood on her brand-new feet praising God and walked with us to the other building where we all ate lunch together.

I told the Fathers, "The feeling to move to Charlotte, North Carolina, went away after the second woman was healed. We flew back home, took our house off the market, and settled back into our old routine with new stories of modern miracles."

The Three Fathers' countenances were ones of grateful faith, and each one expressed his gratitude for my company in their home. I was leaving early in the morning, so I asked them if they would each like a blessing, which I gave them according to what Arcturus had told me to do.

Chapter 24 - Leaving Medellín

I awoke with the sounds of my alarm chiming in the background of my dream. I looked at the clock and it was 3 AM. Maria had washed all my clothing so I packed the night before. All I needed to do was shave and shower.

I jumped in the shower and the water was cold and fresh. It did not warm up, so I completed my shower much more quickly than usual. I dried off and quickly put on my clothes. Time was passing fast, so I put on my socks and shoes, grabbed my bags and headed to the front door. The lock on the door was very unusual, and luckily Father Gabriel had left the key in the lock. As I unlocked the door I could hear steps on the porch. A shorter Colombian man greeted me with "Buenos dias, puedo tragar sus muletas?" Translated, this meant, "Good morning, can I carry your luggage?" I said to him, "Of course, and thank you so much," in Spanish.

He threw my large suitcase up on his shoulder and grabbed my smaller case, a red rolling bag, in his left hand and started heading down the driveway. The path became lit as someone in the house turned on the lights. The entire compound lit up as we descended the stairs, walked down around the archery range, and approached the swimming pool, which I had only enjoyed one time. He opened the trunk and placed my bags inside. He then opened the passenger door asking if I would please get in. I had found a good flight for a good price from Medellín to Bucaramanga on the internet and had printed my tickets the previous evening.

Someone opened the gate and it rolled aside. As we drove through the gate, memories flooded my mind of the kind Fathers who resided inside.

We drove down the usual streets, then turned to the right and connected to a larger road with cars already waking up the city. I could tell this was a new highway; it had fresh pavement and was well lit. It took us up one of the Andes Mountains to a summit high in the trees and descended down into Rio Negro. The airport is very modern, and could have been in any large city in America. The small Colombian man guided the car to the area which said, "Salidas" and parked at the Avianca Airlines terminal. He quickly jumped out and opened my door, popped open the trunk, grabbed my bags, and took them over to the counter where another man checked in my larger bag for my flight. I gave my driver US $10 which he refused, and I was told Father Gabriel had already paid. My flight was leaving at 5 AM and I walked through security quickly and easily, only showing my passport and ticket.

A small café inside the terminal was serving breakfast, so I sat down and ordered eggs over easy and toast. Within minutes, I was eating the freshest eggs with dark orange yolks. The bread, delicious and fresh, had been toasted lightly with fresh butter placed upon it. I used it to mop up the liquid yoke on my plate with ease. A small portion of fresh papaya on a plate had also been placed in front of me. I quickly devoured it knowing the enzymes would help my digestion.

An announcement over the intercom let me know my flight to Bucaramanga was boarding. I grabbed my red rolling bag and headed to my gate. I handed my ticket to the man collecting tickets at the gate, and he said, "Your ticket is wrong," and upgraded my seat to first class. I told him I had not paid for first class, but he said, "Our mutual friend wanted to take care of you."

I entered the plane and sat in row one, seat A. The stewardess asked me, "Would you like some breakfast?" I asked, "What do you have?" She answered, "Father Gabriel said you would like fresh eggs fried in butter, over easy, toast and coffee with some papaya for your digestion." I answered, "I would love to eat exactly that." Within two minutes I was served the same breakfast I had eaten not 15 minutes previously, and somehow I was just as hungry, and it was just as delicious.

I finished my breakfast with delight, as the plane pushed back and the jet engines started to roar. The sun had not yet come over the hill as this beautiful jet roared into the sky, sailing gently over the beautiful Andes Mountains. The electric lights of the city below dimmed, and the light of the sun danced on the forests which appeared below. Smaller cities appeared within these great forests, and disappeared as fast as they could be seen.

Within an hour we were descending through some clouds into Bucaramanga, which was also in the Andes Mountains. The plane touched the runway smoothly, like the touch of Angels, and rolled quickly to stop in front of the terminal at the gate. Everyone moved with great organization, letting the passengers out into the morning sunlight. I collected my bag quickly and easily, then walked out of the terminal into the morning sun.

The summer sun warmed my body as I called Monica Tovar, the only number I still had in my cell phone. The phone rang twice and Monica answered, saying, "Dr. Scott, I'm on my way to the airport to pick you up. I'm only 10 minutes away." I answered, "Thank you so much for picking me up. I will see you in a few minutes."

I waited in the sunlight and I marveled at the beauty of all the flowers planted along the walkways. Before long, a small pickup with two women inside stopped in front of me. Monica told me to get in and put my bag in the back of the truck. Monica introduced me to her sister as we drove away from the airport, then dropped her off 5 minutes later at a beauty salon. We then drove into the city of

Bucaramanga.

The city of Bucaramanga, Colombia, is a modern, beautiful city in the northeastern province. Modern buildings and architecture were everywhere. We drove into an area with beautiful homes and parked. Monica led me over to a courtyard and rang a buzzer. A woman's voice asked, "Who is here?" Monica stated, "It is Monica with Dr. Scott." The lock of the gate buzzed and we opened the door. We walked through many beautiful flowers, a water feature and statues, up to the front door which had also opened. A woman appeared at the front door and welcomed us with handshakes and hugs.

Monica introduced us, and the mistress of the house excitedly invited us in. She asked if I had eaten breakfast, so I told her the story of how I had eaten twice. They laughed at the story and another knock was heard at the front door. A woman entered and I was introduced. She was there to be seen by me and had been told I was a medical intuitive. I started my reading after saying a little prayer. As I began to read I got very strongly that she had been involved in an accident, and that she was being bothered by several dis-incarnated entities. I talked to the entities, saying, "It is time to go to the light, I invite your loved ones and Jesus to guide you back into the light, to take you so you can evolve and move on. You no longer need to be here on this plane. It is time for you to go to the light." There were several entities, two of which expressed fear to me. In answer to their fear, I told them, "You have been lied to and no longer need to be here on the earth. It is time to go back to Heaven and get ready for your next life." I could feel the personalities leave this woman, and the light from her aura cleared. We talked for a few more minutes discussing what had just happened. She noted that she felt different, a good difference, which made her start to cry. I asked her if she would like a blessing, like Arcturus had told me to do.

I started out blessing with the power of the ascended Masters, Jesus and St. Germaine, Melchizedek and Oromisis, Portia and Lady Nada, also calling in the Angels to protect her and watch over her, keeping the negative energies away from her and her loved ones. I blessed her body to receive strength and health, that her bones, joints, ligaments, and tendons would release inflammation and tenderness. I blessed her mind to be strong and healthy. I blessed her relationships to be healed and that peace would return to her life. Then I sealed the blessing upon her in the name of the Father, and of the Son, and of the Holy Spirit, Amen.

She stood up from the chair and grasped me, hugging me tightly, thanking me for healing her. I told her, "You have suffered for a long time and the spirit tells me you are to suffer no more." She thanked me again and I told her not to tell anyone about her healing, but just go out and be happy. She asked if she could pay me, and I told her she could donate whatever she felt the healing was worth and she gave me the equivalent of US $200, which is what I charge in the United States. I told her this was too much but she insisted and said that the feeling she was having was more than worth it. She told me her husband, a neurosurgeon, had been concerned about her for years. She told me her husband would be very happy and that she wanted me to visit with him also.

Another knock came at the door, and another woman entered the room, everyone greeting each other and celebrating. I did another intuitive reading and a blessing upon this woman, who had parasites and fungus invading her brain causing mental instability. As I completed the blessing, clearing her of all the parasitic invaders, she laughed in delight stating that she was seeing more clearly through her eyes than she had for many years.

Monica had scheduled me to meet with six people that morning at the house, which was the home of an architect. After I finished with the intuitive readings and blessings it was lunch time. Monica had arranged lunch at a nearby restaurant. Three of the women who had received readings joined us for lunch, and I told them stories of many other healings.

A delicious lunch was completed and we headed back to the house for additional readings and blessings. I continued into the afternoon, and one of the clients who entered was a Colombian singer and songwriter. His life felt purposeless and he needed to know about his future. I told him he was on his path that was energy-empowered and that he was to impart hope and happiness to the people. I told him that he would intonate the sounds of healing to the country of Colombia. I performed toning on his chakras, intoning the sounds of God into his body. He marveled at the sounds and the qualities within the sounds. He stated, "I want to learn how to do that, which you have done to me, so I can do it for others." I gave him a blessing, saying that the sounds of God, which would come forth out of his mouth, would be for the healing of the people.

He started to cry and said, "You are an answer to my prayers, to know what my purpose is, and now I know." We hugged and I proceeded to explain the sounds, intonation, keys and vowels of the different chakras. He was so happy with the instructions and results of the blessing, he paid me US $200. He also stated that he wanted to do a personal concert for me prior to my leaving Colombia. I told him that was not necessary, but he insisted it would happen.

I continued with several more intuitive readings and blessings, with all of the people receiving benefit. Monica and I then blessed the woman's home where we had been, and the woman asked if I would do toning on her. I proceeded to sing out the sounds of God upon her, starting with the heart chakra in the key of F and the intonation of Om for about five seconds, then moving down to the solar plexus and the key of E, with the intonation of Ong for about five seconds, then moving down to the sacral plexus using the sacred vowels, A, E, I, O, U and the key of D for about nine seconds going through the vowels three times, then going down to the root chakra, the key of C and the intonation of Ahm for about five seconds. I then moved to the throat chakra and the key of G with the intonation of Me for about five seconds and moving the Alpha and Omega with my hands, then up to the third eye with the key of A and the intonation of Ooo. I then moved up to the cerebral chakra with the key of B and the intonation of Ooh and continued up into the higher realms. She especially felt the energy in the higher chakras which made her dance with joy.

She thanked us again for coming, and then we left for the evening, driving the small Toyota pickup back to the south. Monica drove to her mother's nursery, which had many flowers, vegetables, shrubs, trees, and bushes. Monica's mother was a very happy woman and enjoyed working with the plants. She was very knowledgeable about all the various herbs and their uses on the human body. She finished up some paperwork and jumped in the truck with us.

One of the older women who had come for an intuitive reading had invited us over to her house. We drove about a mile from the nursery on a dirt road through an area of heavy vegetation. We entered into the back entrance of a beautiful subdivision and passed several beautiful homes. Stopping at one of the homes, I came to find out this was Monica's mother's home. Monica's mother invited us in and excused herself as she went to change out of her nursery clothing into a fine evening dress.

We then walked over to another beautiful home of a neighbor of Monica's mother, who was married to a project engineer. We rang the doorbell and were greeted by the familiar face of one of the women who had received an intuitive reading. She happily invited us in and walked us through her entrance and living room to where her husband was seated reading some papers. He arose and firmly gripped my hand, thanking me for coming to their house, and expressed the desire to show me his back yard which he had designed.

We went out to a beautiful back yard where many kinds of gorgeous tropical flowers were arranged in lovely settings. There was a large pond, which he proudly stated was filled with the most delicious fish in the region. There was also a second pond filled with trout, which he had brought back from the United States and cultivated. He asked which fish I would like to eat for dinner, and using a net, caught several fish. He then proceeded to throw the fish on a barbecue grill, basting them with butter and sizzling them to perfection.

The women inside had cut up fresh fruit and made a beautiful salad with cucumbers, radishes, and celery. The table had been prepared and we sat down and had the freshest fish I had ever eaten. The meal and the conversation were so delightful. The man of the house told me how he had studied engineering in the United States at Columbia University in New York City, and had come back to Colombia to practice his profession. They had made a wonderful living there in Bucaramanga, but were never able to have children. They were involved in many charities in this area of Colombia.

He asked what I had done with my life, and I started telling him the stories of going to St. Louis University Medical School, working with the law firm defending Monsanto Corporation regarding the chemicals agent orange and dioxin, my further training as an OB/GYN and some of the funny stories of delivering babies. We also talked about my developing stage IV invasive malignant melanoma, the dismal prognosis and my finding the cure through herbal medicine. He seemed very interested in everything I had to say, then told me about his recent diagnosis of osteoarthritis and possible rheumatoid arthritis. He asked which herbs would be the best for treating these things, since the pharmaceutical drugs had caused gastritis and ulcers. I told him about the anti-inflammatory effects of ginger, curcumin, bromelain, and papaya. I also told him of the healing qualities of aloe vera and peppers. As we concluded our conversation, he thanked me for coming to his home. I offered to give him and his home a blessing, which he readily accepted. I anointed this head with olive oil and blessed him, his home and his life with health, abundance and the power and capacity to continue to help all the people in his life and sealed the blessing in the name of the Father, and of the Son, and of the Holy Spirit, Amen.

The energy of the blessing entered into his spirit and he began to cry, thanking me for the blessing. He had to excuse himself because of his emotions, again thanking me for coming to his home to bless him, his wife, and their lives. As we walked out the door, his wife explained that he had become an atheist early on in their marriage, not believing in spirit or in God. She said she felt a shift in his energy as I gave him a blessing, then thanked us again for coming to their home.

We walked Monica's mother back to her house and said good night. We got back into the small Toyota truck, left the subdivision, got onto a large divided highway, and took an exit that led us to a gated community. The guard recognized Monica and exchanged greetings, then we proceeded up the highway to the top of a plateau where we entered a beautiful community of modern houses with beautiful views. Stopping at one of the homes, Monica inserted a key into the locked door and the big wooden door opened. Monica's second sister and her husband owned this beautiful home. Monica had a room on the second story and they led me up to a room on the third story of the home, which was like a suite, with a large bedroom and an opulent window, a large adjoining bathroom, closet, dressing area, tub and separate shower. The plateau where the subdivision had been built was 300 meters above the valley below. The view, even at night in the dark, was astounding. This was to be my room for the next two nights. Monica's niece brought up a pitcher of water and a cup. She asked if there was anything else I needed, showed me where the towels were and politely excused herself.

I had been up since 3 AM that morning. I was feeling quite tired but very fulfilled in what I had done. My heart was full of gratitude to God and the heavens for the beautiful accomplishments that had happened today, with the many blessings I had given people in Bucaramanga. I jumped in the shower, which was delightfully warm, clean and refreshing, kneeled by my bed, said my prayers, thanked the ascended Masters, especially Jesus, the great divine director, and St. Germaine, climbed into the bed, and fell into a deep sleep.

Chapter 25 - Another Day in Bucaramanga

June 12, 2015

I awoke very refreshed the next morning. The sun was coming up in the east and the plateau where the subdivision was located had a gentle slope going down in the east. The subdivision itself had been built in the last 10 years and had many beautiful well-constructed houses, a large park where children were playing already this morning, and beautiful clean streets connecting the homes.

I shaved, got dressed and headed down to the kitchen. The kitchen was beautifully modern with all the latest appliances. Monica's sister was awake and had made coffee, and asked if I would like some. She also asked what I would like for breakfast, so I told her, "I will eat whatever you are accustomed to eating," in Spanish. Monica's sister asked, "Do you like eggs?" I answered, "Yes, fried and over easy." Monica appeared in the kitchen and decided she wanted eggs, too.

Monica told me that she needed to drop her other sister off again as she had no transportation and that she had arranged for me to do more intuitive readings at her mom's nursery that day. We thanked Monica's sister for breakfast and got into the small Toyota truck and drove off in the beautiful Colombian morning.

We drove into a small town off the main highway, an older pueblo with houses which were in disrepair, and picked up Monica's other sister to drive her to the beauty salon where she worked. We then drove over to her mom's nursery and entered the main building. A woman was anxiously waiting for her intuitive reading, so I started my day. There were six people who came that morning and I was able to give them answers to their questions about their health and lives. Each of them was given a blessing according to the spirit. I finished the readings around noon and Monica said, "We will now go to another house where I've got several other people wanting to meet with you. But first we will feed you lunch." Monica's mother had prepared a beautiful meal with fresh tropical fruit and sandwiches. When we finished the lunch, we said our goodbyes and headed out to the small Toyota truck. We ended up in another beautiful subdivision and stopped at a home with beautiful tropical trees and landscaping.

We rang the doorbell, and a middle-aged woman answered the door, greeting us with, "Good afternoon. I am so glad you have come." We entered a beautifully furnished home and there was another knock on the door as my next appointment arrived. I did intuitive readings and gave several more blessings the entire afternoon. There was a spirit of peace, joy, and bliss. Many of the people we saw were a part of the Transcendental Meditation movement and very successful in their business and home lives. They were all very grateful for the information and blessings.

When the day was completed, Monica gave me all the donations of money, which was more than I had paid for my entire trip to Colombia and Bucaramanga. I marveled how the ascended Masters had taken such good care of me on this trip. We thanked the woman whose home had been opened up for the readings, gave her personal information and blessed her and her home, jumped in the small Toyota truck and headed to the nursery to pick up Monica's mother.

Back at Monica's mother's house, she prepared us an evening meal with fresh tropical fruit, organic vegetables, and chicken and rice. Monica's mother asked for an intuitive reading also, which I did for her and gave her a blessing. She was very grateful and insisted on paying me, but I told her, "I am grateful to do it for the price of the beautiful meal you prepared."

When we had finished our meal and conversation, we got back in the little Toyota truck and drove up to the gated subdivision high on the plateau. When we arrived, Monica's sister had heard about the wonderful intuitive readings and blessings and desired for me to do one for her. So we sat down and I tuned into her body, health and guides and proceeded to give her answers to her questions and information about her life. At the end, I placed my hands upon her head and gave her a blessing from the ascended Masters, in the name of the Father and of the Son and of the Holy Spirit.

As I prepared for sleep, Monica knocked on the door and told me, "The neural surgery doctor and his wife want to invite you to a party tomorrow at their home. The musician who was healed wants to give you a private concert at the party." I answered, "Yes, I would very much like that, but I have to be at the airport by 2:30 PM." Monica bid me good night and I settled in to my bed thinking, "Thank you, thank you." I opened the window to a fresh cool breeze entering into the lofted room. That night I had many beautiful dreams.

Chapter 26 - My Final Day in Colombia

June 13, 2015

I awoke to the beautiful sound of tropical birds. I looked out the window and there were several macaw birds, chattering delightfully. It had rained during the night, making the air wonderfully fresh. Sun was shining brightly down upon the beautiful tropical subdivision.

I got up and dressed and went down the stairs to the kitchen. Monica's sister had already brewed up some delightful coffee and fried up some eggs just the way I liked them. Papaya, pineapple, and passion fruit were cut up and placed on the table. Breakfast was delicious and I thanked her.

I went upstairs and packed my bags since I was leaving to go back to the United States. I brought my bags downstairs to find Monica eating her breakfast. She finished up and I gave my farewell to Monica's sister and thanked her for allowing me to stay in her home. I took my bags out and put them in the back of the Toyota pickup. We said our farewells again with hugs, got into the truck and drove down the plateau.

Monica desired for me to say goodbye to her mother, so we drove down to the subdivision, picked up her mother and took her to the nursery. Monica's mother had raised a very spiritual family and all of her children meditated. The nursery had been run by her husband, but when he died Monica's mother took over the business. She supported her children with this business and had done very well. She asked if I could bless the business, which I did, with the ascended Masters' help.

We then drove the small Toyota pickup to a beautiful subdivision with a wall around it and a gated entry. Monica buzzed the gate and the neural surgeon gave permission for us to enter. It was a beautiful subdivision, with many beautiful homes with gated courtyards, manicured yards and swimming pools. We drove up to a two-story house, parked the car and approached the entrance. The doctor met us at the entrance and invited us in with a big grin on his face. He thanked me for coming to Bucaramanga to bless his wife and was very grateful for the changes in her health and demeanor. He said the day was to honor me and he was grateful to have me in his home.

I found out later that he had trained in the United States for his medical education and residency. Many of the doctors in Bucaramanga trained in the finest medical schools in the United States and returned to Colombia to transform the medical care for the entire country. Bucaramanga was known throughout South America to have the best doctors and medical facilities on the continent. He introduced me to his daughter, who was completing medical school in the United States and had been accepted as an OB/GYN resident to complete her studies. He was happy to learn I had also been an OB/GYN in the United States and wanted me to talk to her. We spent about 30 minutes discussing her life, and I gave her an intuitive reading, which answered many of her questions. Being doctors and scientists, they were amazed that I had the spiritual ability to answer their questions in an open, truthful manner. They asked how I had been able to do this and I told them about my near-death experiences and the stage IV cancer that had almost taken my life. They were amazed I had survived and thrived.

The famous Colombian musician who received an intuitive reading on my first day in Bucaramanga arrived and his band set up their equipment. A female vocalist had also come, and another male accompanist, who played the piano, set up his equipment. We all gathered in a bungalow out by the pool and the band began to play, singing beautiful harmony both in Spanish and English.

They played for two hours, then we all sat down to a meal of seafood and tropical fruit. It was a fiesta celebrating the blessings which I had brought to Bucaramanga. Soon it was time to go to the airport, so I said my goodbyes and hugged everyone. Monica and I left in the pickup and drove to the airport quickly and easily. I checked my bags and waited near the gate at a small restaurant with a big screen TV showing a soccer game of Colombia versus Brazil. I boarded the plane on time and flew to the Bogotá airport where I had a one-hour layover, and finally boarded a large, wide-body United Airline jet. I was on my way home.

We arrived at the Houston airport at around 6 AM. I gathered my luggage at the baggage claim and reentered the United States of America. I have always been a patriot for my country and freedom. I was so grateful to be home. I went through customs and proceeded to the gate which would take me back to Denver, Colorado, and then to St. George, Utah.

I arrived at the St. George airport to find Vicki, and my daughters Cloie and Sofie waiting for me at the gate. We collected my luggage and went home.

Chapter 27 - Living in a Carbon-Based World with Many on Drugs

On the morning of October 17, 2016, St Germaine said, "I want you to add the following to the book of Padre Gabriel:

"When the DNA was created and human beings were created, beginning to think, create and decipher the universe and become the spark of God, there was a relationship between the seven Elohim and the seven Rays of light from God. The seven Chakras within the human body became interconnected with the seven Rays of light, the glands of the body and the links between the various nerved plexi of the nervous system of the body.

"Neurotransmitters or chemical messengers that send signals between nerve cells, allowing the brain and the nervous system to communicate, are mostly manufactured in the hypothalamus and amygdala, and these chemicals are passed to the pituitary gland and pineal gland. These neuropeptides, also known as ligands, then stimulate the production of hormones, which are responsible for emotions and feelings being created within the human body, stimulating the various organs to help them do their jobs.

"These hormones then stimulate the Chakra associated with the emotion and energize the creative thoughts manifesting the intent with the emotion. The plexus of nerves and the neuropeptides then create a vortex of creative energy, creating energy and the stimulation of light, manifesting the atomic structure into existence. Therefore, when we have a thought, it reflects instantly in our auric field with light energy. It then stimulates the emotion or energy within the organs which are associated with the various Chakras involved and encrypt and store the various emotions and creative energies.

"In the beginning the thoughts and emotions were pure and positive, producing pure and positive creations. When the first negative emotions and thoughts began through deviating from the thoughts of God, negative creations began to appear and manifest. This began the duality of creation, one negative thought, emotion, manifestation and creation at a time.

"Homo Luminous started to manifest into lower density and became Homo Sapiens, and the living planets on which they lived became denser and less hospitable for spontaneous manifestation.

"In our modern era, with science becoming the religion and main belief system, man started to create pharmaceutical and artificial treatments. Organic and inorganic substances began to be created by the scientists, with both good effects and side effects (bad), leaving behind the healing natural remedies and concoctions of the plant kingdom.

"Instead of healing the body, various substances and drugs altering natural substances became prevalent. Opioids from the poppy plants became popular as mood, and body-altering substances for pain and emotional disconnection.

"Throughout the early nineteenth century, the recreational use of opium throughout the world grew, and by 1830, the British dependence on the drug reached an all-time high. The British sent warships to the coast of China in 1839 in response to China's attempt to suppress the opium traffic, beginning the 'First Opium War.'

"Morphine was first extracted from opium in a pure form in the early nineteenth century. Morphine, the most active substance in opium, is a very powerful painkiller that addicted many US Civil War soldiers. It was used widely as a painkiller during the mid-1860's through the second World War, and many soldiers became addicted.

"Codeine, a less powerful drug that is found in opium but can be synthesized (man-made), was first isolated in 1830 in France by Jean-Pierre Robiquet, to replace raw opium for medical purposes. It was used mainly as a liquid cough and mild pain remedy, and later was made into pills mixed with aspirin and became Tylenol.

"Codeine, a scientific alteration of the opioids, also began to be abused. Heroin became the next altered substance, highly addictive, enslaving and damaging to the human spirit.

"In 1874, chemists trying to find a less addictive form of morphine made heroin. Heroin had twice the potency of morphine, but a shorter half-life, and heroin use and addiction soon became a serious problem. It was found that the drug was so addictive, enslavement and control of humans could be induced with the use of the drug, having it even enslave women and men to prostitution.

"Coca is one of the oldest, most potent and most dangerous stimulants of natural origin. Three thousand years before the birth of Christ, ancient Incas in the Andes chewed coca leaves to get their hearts racing and to speed their breathing to counter the effects of living in thin mountain air.

"Native Peruvians chewed coca leaves only during religious ceremonies. This taboo was broken when Spanish soldiers invaded Peru in 1532. Forced Indian laborers in Spanish silver mines were kept supplied with coca leaves because it made them easier to control and exploit.

"And then, from the South American continent, it was found that by alkalizing coca leaves, cocaine could be produced, which was an easier to use drug and highly stimulating to the brain, nervous system and Chakra systems. Cocaine was first isolated (extracted from coca leaves) in 1859 by German chemist Albert Niemann. It was not until the 1880's that it started to be popularized in the medical community.

"Austrian psychoanalysis founder Sigmund Freud, who used the drug himself, was the first to broadly promote cocaine as a tonic to cure depression and sexual impotence. In 1884, he published an article entitled 'Über Coca' (About Coke) which promoted the 'benefits' of cocaine, calling it a 'magical' substance.

"Freud, however, was not an objective observer. He used cocaine regularly, prescribed it to his girlfriend and his best friend and recommended it for general use.

"While noting that cocaine had led to 'physical and moral decadence,' Freud kept promoting cocaine to his close friends, one of whom ended up suffering from paranoid hallucinations with 'white snakes creeping over his skin.'

"He also believed that, 'For humans the toxic dose (of cocaine) is very high, and there seems to be no lethal dose.' Contrary to this belief, one of Freud's patients died from a high dosage he prescribed.

"In 1886, the popularity of the drug got a further boost when John Pemberton included coca leaves as an ingredient in his new soft drink, Coca-Cola. The euphoric and energizing effects on the consumer helped to skyrocket the popularity of Coca-Cola by the turn of the century.

"From the 1850's to the early 1900's, cocaine and opium-laced elixirs (magical or medicinal potions), tonics and wines were broadly used by people of all social classes. Notable figures who promoted the 'miraculous' effects of cocaine tonics and elixirs included inventor Thomas Edison and actress Sarah Bernhardt. The drug became popular in the silent film industry and the pro-cocaine messages coming out of Hollywood at that time influenced millions.

"Cocaine use in society increased and the dangers of the drug gradually became more evident. Public pressure forced the Coca-Cola company to remove the cocaine from the soft drink in 1903.

"By 1905, it had become popular to snort cocaine and within five years, hospitals and medical literature had started reporting cases of nasal damage resulting from the use of this drug.

"In 1912, the United States government reported 5,000 cocaine-related deaths in one year and by 1922, the drug was officially banned from public use.

"In the 1970's, cocaine emerged as the fashionable new drug for entertainers and businesspeople. Cocaine seemed to be the perfect companion for a trip into the fast lane. It 'provided energy' and helped people stay 'up.'

"In the 1970's through the present time, the United States Corporate Military Complex (secret government), seeing the potential of capitalizing on the enormous profit potential to fund clandestine operations, began to contract raw materials, production, transportation, and distribution of cocaine alkaloid, causing use, prices, and profits to soar.

"These chemically altered drugs and alcohol can be used in combination, which powerfully affects each energy center in the body. Alcohol primarily dampens the emotional center of the solar plexus. Many people drink to dampen their emotional center and think that they are relaxing and helping these emotional centers, but actually, we can damage the organs and protection around the auric field, to allow parasites, disembodied and previously embodied spirits, demons and other entities into the auric fields."

St. Germaine continued, "Opioids, heroin, cocaine and inhalants also dampen and affect the brain through the third eye (mid brain, pituitary) and cerebral chakra (pineal gland), and also the heart chakra (lungs, heart, thymus) and solar plexus (liver, pancreas, spleen), with the associated damage to those organs. When used frequently, they can also increase damage to the 'Love Center' of the heart, triple

157

warmer, thymus, and lungs.

"Cocaine in its alkaloid form also stimulates the lower sacral sexual plexus and root plexus of nerves and hormones causing over-stimulation of the adrenals, sexual glands and the kidneys. It also drives the cranial nerves of the third eye and throat chakra to be overstimulated, causing over-stimulation of the senses of hearing, seeing, taste, smell and tactile sensation through the skin.

"This over-stimulation causes addictive neuropeptide formation for the 'high' that it produces which causes the individual to seek a constant restimulation of these organs and systems. There is a similar reaction with heroin and the opioid substances which are abused by millions on the planet. All of these substances create disharmony in the nervous system, the nerve plexus, the associated emotional centers, and the organ systems of the body, storing dangerous emotions and memories which cause damage to the tissues, disease and addiction.

"Father Gabriel's pure intention of love created the attention to resolving the addictive tendencies, emotional and physical traumas and healing the auric fields and chakras of the physical, emotional, mental, and spiritual bodies. This essentially reverses all the damages done from the chemicals used, and the emotions felt by the children and young adults and older adults essentially changes their emotional state back to a state of emotional healing, forgiveness, gratitude, and love."

Chapter 28 - Exploring the Psyche

Sigmund Freud - Psychoanalysis

The fascinating information below has been mostly pulled from an online article written by S.A. McLeod titled, *Sigmund Freud.* McLeod, S. A. (2013). Retrieved from www.simplypsychology.org/Sigmund-Freud.html

Sigmund Freud explored the human mind and became the father of modern psychoanalysis. His contributions to psychology are vast. Freud was one of the most influential people of the 20th century and his enduring legacy has influenced not only psychiatry and psychology, but also art, literature and even the way people bring up their children. Freud's lexicon has become embedded within the vocabulary of Western society and the words he introduced through his theories are now being used by everyday people, such as personality types, libido, denial, repression, cathartic, Freudian slip, histrionic and neurotic.

Freud believed that when we explain our own behavior to others or ourselves, self-protection affects our conscious mental activity so that we rarely give a true account of our motivation. This is not because we are deliberately lying. Human beings are great deceivers of others, and are even more adept at self deception. Our rationalization of our conduct, disguising the real reasons for our behavior, dominated Freud's life work.

Psychoanalysis is often known as the talking cure. Freud would encourage his patients to talk freely and truthfully regarding their symptoms, neurosis or psychosis and to describe exactly what was on their mind. Freud's theories included the following:

The unconscious mind. Freud from the years 1900 through 1905 developed a topographical model of the mind, where he describes the features of the mind's structure and function. Freud used the analogy of an iceberg to describe the three levels of the mind. On the surface is consciousness which consists of those thoughts that are the focus of our attention in the now, and this is seen as the tip of the iceberg. The second level is the preconscious which consists of all that can be retrieved from memory. The third and most significant region is the unconscious. Here lies the processes that are the real cause of most behavior. Like an iceberg, the most important part of the mind is a part you cannot see. The unconscious mind acts as a repository, a cauldron of primitive wishes and impulses kept at bay and mediated by the preconscious area. Freud found later that some events and desires were often too frightening or painful for his patients to acknowledge, and Freud believed such information was locked away in the unconscious mind for self protection. This can happen through the process of repression. Freud emphasized the importance of the unconscious mind. He stated that the unconscious mind governs behavior to a greater degree than people suspect, and the goal of psychoanalysis is to make the unconscious mind conscious.

The psyche. By 1923 Freud developed a more structural model of the mind comprised of the entities id, ego, and superego (what Freud called the psychic apparatus). These are not physical areas within the brain but rather hypothetical conceptualizations with important medical functions. Freud assumed that id operated at an unconscious level according to the pleasure principle or gratification from satisfying basic instincts. The id comprises two kinds of biological instincts or drives which Freud called "Eros" and "Thanatos." Eros, or life instinct, helps the individual to survive; it directs life-sustaining activities such as respiration, eating, and sex. The energy created by the life instincts

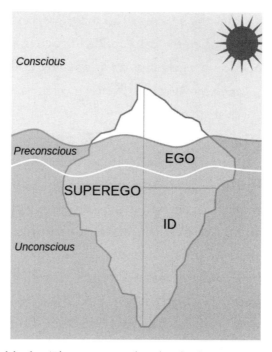

is known as libido. Thanatos or the death distinct is viewed as a set of destructive forces present in all human beings. When this energy is directed onto others, it is expressed as aggression and violence. Freud believed that the Eros is stronger than the Thanatos, thus enabling people to survive rather than self-destruct. The ego develops from the id during infancy, with the ego's goal to satisfy the demands of the id in a socially acceptable way. In contrast to the id, the ego follows the reality principle, as it operates in both the conscious and unconscious mind. The superego develops during early childhood, when the child identifies with the same-sex parent, and is responsible for ensuring moral standards are followed. The superego operates on the morality principle and motivates us to behave in a socially responsible and acceptable manner. The basic dilemma of all human existence is that each element of the psychic apparatus makes demands upon us that are incompatible with the other two. Inner conflict is inevitable. An example of this is that the superego can make a person feel guilty if rules are not followed when there is a conflict between the goals of the id and superego, and the ego must act as a referee and mediate this conflict. The ego can deploy various defense mechanisms to prevent it from becoming overwhelmed by anxiety.

Psychosexual stages. During the Victorian era in which Freud lived and worked, women, in particular, were forced to repress their sexual needs. In many cases the result was some form of neurotic illness. Freud sought to understand the nature and variety of these illnesses by retracing the sexual history of his patients. This was not primarily an investigation into the sexual experiences, as such, but far more important were the patient's wishes and desires, their experience of love, hate, shame, guilt, and fear – and how they handled these powerful emotions. This is what led to the most controversial part of Freud's work – his theory of psychosexual development and of the Oedipus complex. (For more information on these stages, please research Freud's theory of psychosexual development.)

Dream analysis. Freud considered dreams to be the road to the unconscious. Dreams were the ego's defenses and the way that some of the individual's repressed material could come through to awareness, albeit in distorted form. Freud distinguished between the manifest content of the dream and the latent content, the symbolic meaning of the dream or the underlying wish. The manifest content was often based on the events of the day, and the purpose of dream work was to transform the forbidden, underlying wish of the dream into a non-threatening desire, thus reducing anxiety and allowing us to sleep. He also discussed the process of condensation in dreams, which is enjoining two or more ideas/images; for example, a dream about a house might be a combination of worries about security, as well as worries about one's appearance to the rest of the world. This takes place when we transform the person or object we are really concerned about into someone or something else. Freud also did other work with dreams, creating "Dream Analysis." Freud was followed by many psychiatrists, psychologists, and social workers who formed the Vienna Psychoanalytic Society [1908].

Carl Jung - Psychotherapy

The information in quotes below is from an online article titled, *Carl Jung: Archetypes and Analytical Psychology*. The entire article can be read online here: https://www.psychologistworld.com/cognitive/ carl-jung-analytical-psychology.php

Carl Jung created an idea of personal unconscious and a collective unconscious which included various archetypes. "An archetype is the model image of a person or role, and includes the mother figure, father figure, wise old man, clown/joker, and others." Carl Jung found that we each embody with a primary archetype and secondary archetypes.

Carl Jung also noted that each one of us has "a persona or an identity that we wish to project to others. He used the Latin term persona, which can refer either to a person's personality with the mask of an actor, intentionally, or the persona can be constructed from archetypes in the collective unconscious, or be influenced by ideas of social roles in society."

As the persona is not a true reflection of our consciousness, but rather an idealized image which people aspire to, inner conflicts and a repression of our own personality can conflict with the persona, or the acting role. With this repression of our true identity, drug use or identification with the defective personality traits can supersede the higher consciousness.

Carl Jung also described the shadow archetype, which "is composed primarily of the elements of ourselves that we consider to be negative. The shadow may contain many repressed ideas and thoughts which we do not wish to integrate into our outward persona," but these have a tendency to surface when we are in uncertainty, or a weakened state of mind.

He also developed the anima/animus archetypes which represent the opposite gender to a person's core personality. "As a person develops a gender identity, such as that of being male, they repress the aspects of their personality which might be considered to be feminine, such as empathy in social situations." The anima and animus are idealized impressions of the male or female, which emerge from the collective unconscious and charge our ideas of the opposite gender. In today's society, gender identification is becoming more socialized and obscure.

Carl Jung also theorized and identified the introvert and extrovert personality types. The introvert, though quiet and unsociable, takes the time to think over problems and makes better choices than the extrovert who acts spontaneously and doesn't always think about his actions.

Father Gabriel, in his work helping children to get off the streets and recover from severe dysfunctional, social situations, has found that gender identity becomes a much more important archetypal construct. He openly works with these children, letting them safely develop the gender identity to which they are attracted most and insures the other children allow them to identify without judgment.

This creates a safe environment for progression and education. Father Gabriel found Carl Jung much more compassionate with his theories of psychotherapy, as opposed to Sigmund Freud, who addressed humans with more animalistic qualities and base desires.

Viktor Frankl - Miracle of Logotherapy

The information in quotes below is from an online article titled, *Carl Jung: Archetypes and Analytical Psychology*. The entire article can be read online here: https://www.psychologistworld.com/cognitive/carl-jung-analytical-psychology.php

Father Gabriel stated, "One of the miracles in my life was going to Europe in the year 1987 and attending an international symposium of psychologists in Vienna, Austria," a conference which, Father Gabriel says, "changed my life forever."

Victor Frankel, a survivor of the Holocaust and author of *Man's Search for Meaning*, spoke and presented a new psychiatric therapy that he termed "logotherapy," which is based on the premise that the human being is motivated by a "will to meaning," an inner desire to find a meaning in his or her life. The following excerpts are from www.logotherapyinstitute.org/about_logotherapy.html:

There are three basic tenets of logotherapy:

1. Life has meaning under all circumstances, even the most miserable ones.

2. Our main motivation for living is our will to find our life purpose.

3. We have freedom of choice in finding meaning in what we do and what we experience, or at least in the stand we take when faced with a situation of unchangeable suffering.

The human spirit referred to in logotherapy as defined by Viktor Frankl is that which is uniquely human in each one of us. Though in no way opposed to religion, the term is not used in a religious sense. Victor Frankel taught, "We can discover this meaning in three different ways."

1. By creating a work or doing a deed.

2. By experiencing something or encountering someone.

3. By the attitude we take toward unavoidable suffering; that is, "Everything can be taken from a man but one thing: the last of human freedoms, to choose one's attitude in any given set of circumstances."

Assumptions:

1. The human being is an entity consisting of body, mind, and spirit.

2. Life has meaning under all circumstances, even the most miserable.

3. The human being has a will to meaning.

4. The human being has freedom under all circumstances to activate the will to find meaning.

5. Life has a demand quality to which people must respond if decisions are to be meaningful.

6. The individual is unique.

The first assumption deals with the body (soma), mind (psyche), and spirit (noos). According to Viktor Frankl, the body and mind are what we have, and in the spirit is what we are.

The second assumption is "ultimate meaning." This is difficult to grasp but it is something everyone experiences and it represents an universal order, the universal world with laws and truth that go beyond human laws and truth.

The third assumption is seen as our main motivation for living and acting. When we see our meaning, we are ready for any type of suffering. This is considered to be different than our will to achieve power and pleasure.

The fourth assumption is that we are free to activate our will to find meaning and this can be done under any circumstances. This deals with change of attitudes about an unavoidable fate. Frankel was able to test the first four assumptions when he was confined in the concentration camps, observing all the people, all those incarcerated as prisoners, the guards and the German captors.

The fifth assumption, the meaning of the moment, is more practical with daily living than ultimate meaning (finding purpose with life). Unlike ultimate meaning, this meaning can be found and fulfilled. This can be done by following the values of family or society, or by following the voice of our conscience. We still make a choice in this assumption.

The sixth assumption deals with one's sense of meaning. This is enhanced by the realization that we are irreplaceable and unique. It recognizes the spark of life (from the great beyond or God) in each one of us.

In essence, all humans are unique with an entity of body, mind, and spirit. We all go through unique situations and are constantly looking to find meaning. We are free to do this at all times in response to certain demands and situations.

Logotherapy, which represents finding our meaning, "is a life-oriented existential philosophy and therapy which has been expanded by therapists throughout the world, working in counseling, education, medicine, nursing, psychology, social work, and other fields where the question of the meaning of life and one's particular purpose becomes pertinent," according to the International Forum for Logotherapy.

Joseph Fabry, JD, who fled from Nazi Austria in 1938 to the United States, heard Viktor Frankl speak at a lecture at a Unitarian church of Berkeley, California, which changed Joseph Fabry's perspective on life. He became quick friends with Viktor Frankl, and wrote the book Guideposts to Meaning, which helped disseminate Viktor Frankl's logotherapy for the English-speaking world, particularly the North American mentality.

In 1977, Joseph Fabry was one of the facilitators of a two-day celebration with Viktor Frankl in the Zellerbach auditorium of the University of California campus in Berkeley. Viktor Frankl was given the Albert Schweitzer Reverence of Life award, and was told he had single handedly re-humanized psychotherapy and psychoanalysis. Viktor dared to "introduce the human spirit into therapy and to make the resources of the human spirit 'the medicine chest of mental health.'" Survivor of four Nazi prison camps, Dr. Frankl responded, "I accept this award as a witness to what might be considered as history's most monstrous violation of reverence of life."

Mystics and Adepts of the Mysteries knew that beyond our five physical senses there is a higher intelligence. They called this intelligence the logos, or the divine blueprint. Followers of Jesus later translated this term as "the word," teachings of God, the breath of life, intelligence of God or the Holy Spirit. This energy created the universe and the knowledge and power from that creative intelligence can assist every human being. Scientists have referred to this intelligence as the "Unified Field" or "Universal Intelligence."

Viktor Frankl recognized this divine intelligence while in the concentration camps during World War II. He also recognized that sodium fluoride put into the water supplies of the concentration camps made this intelligence more difficult to access, making the people more docile and easier to manipulate. It has been found that sodium fluoride is being added to our water supply here in the United States, despite many municipalities voting to remove this poison.

Dr. Frankl utilized the logos in his logotherapy, making his patients aware of their higher intelligence, helping each individual to understand their own purpose in life. He found this was very useful in bringing about positive changes in the personality of each person.

This is the fundamental difference between Viktor Frankl's logotherapy, the psychoanalysis of Sigmund Freud and psychotherapy of Carl Jung.

Chapter 29 - The Pineal Gland

The pineal gland, also called the pineal body, is a small (<8 mm) endocrine gland located in the mid-part of the brain. It produces the hormone melatonin from serotonin, which affects the modulation of the wake cycle and photo-periodic seasonal function. It is tucked in between the cerebral hemispheres of the brain where the two rounded thalamic bodies join.

The pineal gland, or pineal body, is located between the two hemispheres of the cerebrum of our brain. It produces melatonin from serotonin, and a substance called DMT (N,N-Dimethyltryptamine), a psychoactive or "psychedelic" hormone important in the dream and visionary state of the human brain. (The modern word "psychedelic" refers to psychoactive drugs whose primary action is to alter cognition and perception.) It has been found through scientific studies that sodium fluoride calcifies the pineal gland causing less production of all the hormones of the pineal gland. This causes poor sleep, depression and lack of motivation, dreams, and visionary thinking. Father Gabriel uses the flower essence of the bird of paradise because it stimulates the pineal gland, allowing it to produce DMT, restore better sleep and dream states, and help humans access higher states of consciousness, or logos.

Chapter 30 - Father Gabriel on Meditation

Meditation assists oxygenation and stimulation of the brain and glands of the brain, including the pineal gland. It has been shown through studies, including scientific studies, that meditation is very beneficial to the health of human beings by reducing high blood pressure, depression and anxiety. It reduces anger, hatred, grief, shame, blame, and other negative emotions. Meditation has been shown to increase awareness and consciousness of others. Many individuals who start practicing meditation have more tolerance, compassion, understanding of the self, and experiences of bliss and transcendence.

Father Gabriel was taught Transcendental Meditation by Deepak Chopra in 1975, one of many types of meditation available at the time. He became a practitioner of Transcendental Meditation, finding it soothing to his soul and bringing more bliss into his life.

Father Gabriel found it so effective in bringing joy and bliss to himself that he decided to teach the technique to prisoners he would visit in the prison system, people suffering from their "sins." He found it very effective in calming their souls and bringing enlightenment with spiritual growth. It also effectively brought a deeper understanding of issues facing criminals, giving them further insight into their lives and habits.

He decided to start teaching children the technique in his parish. He found that it helped the children find peace and their purpose in life, which was very helpful for those who had lost their way, especially the children who were abandoned in the streets and had become drug addicts, and/or had been sexually abused through prostitution. It produced self-reflection, helped them abandon addictive behavior, helped them with forgiveness of others and forgiveness of self, and gave them a desire for self-improvement and to move forward in their lives.

When I visited Father Gabriel, he described many beautiful experiences of the children who had been changed by Transcendental Meditation. His emotions were very close to the surface and tears swelled up in his eyes. You could feel his love and compassion for the children. His voice quivered with emotion. His body language shifted to that of an ascended Master. I felt like I was in the presence of a modern day saint as he described the changes in the lives of the children.

My time with the Three Fathers will be one of the most precious memories of my existence, comparable to my marriages and births of all my children. Living with these honorable men, listening to their advanced theology, experiencing their love and passion as they moved through a tumultuous world expanded my own vision of what the world can be.

My life has been enriched immensely from traveling to the various Hogares Claret and experiencing the beautiful souls who were progressing in conscious expansion and love consciousness, becoming God's children because of the love of these evolved, saintly priests.

We who live in America, the land of the free and the home of the brave, should quiet our minds with meditation. We should let love, not violence, be our desire. Let joy and bliss pump through our arteries and veins, not drugs. Let compassion, not revenge and hate, fill our souls.

As we move into the age of Aquarius, let us remember who we really are, sons and daughters of a beautiful universe and a compassionate loving God.

Chapter 31 - Summary with Father Gabriel

Father Gabriel stated, "We have spent 28 years working for the dignity, love and life of the children of the streets. With the Hogares Claret, the treatment begins with love.

"Many times, desperate families leave their children in the streets. The mother or father ends their life in suicide or dies from drugs, or the war. Sometimes because their parents were desperate, not having money or the capacity to care for their children, the children end up in the streets, barefoot and poorly dressed, without shelter or food.

"We find children working as prostitutes. We find children working at bars and other places, boys and girls involved in child prostitution. This encourages their subjugation and abuse by the population. Many start using inhalants or other inexpensive drugs to forget their life situation.

"With Hogares Claret, we give the children a new beginning. We give them food, warmth, shelter, clothing, and safety, providing the basic human needs. But we go further than that. We provide education and dignity, teach them how to be good citizens, and elevate them to find their purpose in life.

"And why do they come to Hogares Claret? 'I don't have a family, my mother was killed, ... my father was killed, ... I'm alone. My grandmother or grandfather brought me and left me.' Many run away from a bad situation.

"When the children come to us and ask to be removed from their life in the streets voluntarily, we never force them to better their lives. We never take them by force. It is their choice. The basic therapy is love. Love is the empirical medicine for any illness or disorder. When the child feels they are welcome and loved, when a child feels an adult or educator is concerned about them, the child who came from the violence and the hostility of the street, from being mistreated, and who sees aggression and became aggressive, through this love, miracles happen. The child changes. The child evolves. We can change the abandoned child or young adult, heal those feelings of being discarded and abandoned, and help them become a product of acceptance, compassion and love."

Father Gabriel continues, "I am convinced that a child is not a problem. A child is an opportunity. A child has infinite potential. A child is like a shrine, a temple, a sanctuary. A child is like a dance of creation. We know a child accepts help because of what we call resilience, or the capacity of the child to be reborn continuously. We know that a child can accept that love and transition into a life of dignity and service.

"We, as teachers can help, because of what we call the resilience of youth, the capacity of children to be retaught. When a child starts to practice yoga, or Transcendental Meditation every day, morning and evening, when a child closes their eyes and begins to meditate, when a child practices the Siddhis, they open themselves up to a field of infinite possibilities. The world opens up for the child and the child discovers their essential nature, which is love."

Father Gabriel then quoted Maharishi and said, "The world opens up for the child, and then the child discovers the unified field of consciousness, of infinite possibilities, and hope and bliss follow."

Father Gabriel continues, "I have seen thousands of children go through the foundation, and every case is unique and fascinating, to see what state of mind and spirit a child arrives at Hogares Claret in, and see the transformation, how they become a healed human being, a human with infinite potential. That is very gratifying for me.

"I think that we are all committed to transforming the world where we're living. We have to leave a better world than the one we found. I believe in solidarity, unity. I believe the solution is within every person and child, within each human being. In each one of us there is a sanity in the moment we take refuge, there in the moment, when we enter the 'field of infinite Love.' Solutions come from every person, every loving person, and when we put them altogether, there are many warriors. We all must globalize love."

Each day I spent with the three Catholic Fathers was one of the greatest blessings and events of my life. This book is dedicated to their loving dedication.

Chapter 32 - Mystery of the Harbinger

St. Germaine wanted me to add this chapter to assist people seeking truth.

The Harbinger, written by Jonathan Cahn, tells a story of a prophet visiting with a writer. The story covers several years after the tragedy of the twin towers and September 11, 2001.

The Harbinger was written as a warning to America, specifically the United States of America as one of the world powers. It describes how the United States of America was founded on the principles of Judeo-Christian law. The founding fathers, authors of the Constitution, writers of the Declaration of Independence and the early Congress, Senators and lawmakers built a country founded upon the principle that all men are created equal under the laws of a supreme being.

Through the years, those laws were changed and the Constitution trampled on. Corporate America was born on the backs of the working people. Freedom of religion and spiritual choice became a hiss and a byword. Theological and spiritual studies were replaced with sports, science, and the pursuit of money and pleasure. Family values were replaced with selfishness, self-gratification and base desires. Computers and devices replaced human to human communication.

Because of this, America, which had been a chosen land and had prospered among all other lands, now had come under condemnation because a majority of the people chose not to follow God or even believe in God. Prayer was banned in the schools and all public gatherings and meetings, replaced for a moment of silence to get your Coca-Cola and snacks.

The main character in *The Harbinger*, Nouriel Kaplan, has a discussion with a woman named Anna Goren about ancient mysteries and secrets. Nouriel tells of his meetings with a prophet and their many discussions about harbingers and the seals associated with the harbingers, beginning with the attack on the towers of September 11, 2001, and all of the major stock market crashes and wars since that time.

Nouri brings a recording device during sessions and discussions with the prophet, and records all of what he is told. The prophet gives him seals, or messages and he must figure out what it means.

The first harbinger: the breach. The prophet describes the breach as allowing the enemy to penetrate the land, or kingdom, on which God's people reside. The breach means God's protection is removed so that the enemy can strike within their own land.

The second harbinger: terrorist. In ancient Israel, it was the ancient Assyrians who began to attack them from within their borders, and then continued to attack and infiltrate their lands. The breach encouraged the Assyrians, so they continued to attack Israel. The correlation to America is that the descendants of the ancient Assyrians were the ones who planned to attack the United States of America as an act of terrorism.

The third harbinger: the fallen bricks. The bricks were part of Isaiah 9:10, meaning that the World Trade Center, a symbol of America's economic power, had been destroyed. [Isaiah 9:10 states: The bricks are fallen down, but we will build with hewn stones: the sycamores are cut down, but we will change them into cedars.]

Fourth harbinger: the tower. The bricks had fallen, but we rebuilt with hewn stone a tower that was stronger, better, and taller than before. It was called the Freedom Tower.

The fifth harbinger: the 'Gazit' stone. This is a stone, quarried, chiseled and carved out of mountain rock. A mountain matching the ancient mountain near Israel was here in America near New York City, and it was here that they quarried the Gazit stone. The stone was placed at Ground Zero for the rebuilding of the Freedom Tower. It was a message of defiance to the judgments of God. Just as ancient Israel had rebuilt after the attack of the Assyrians, here in America we rebuilt the tower as a message of defiance to our enemies.

The sixth harbinger: the Sycamore. The Sycamore tree is also known as a big mulberry tree. At Ground Zero, the Sycamore tree that had been there for years had been planted by the founding fathers of the United States of America. In the same area, a statue of George Washington, the first president of the United States of America, stands on Wall Street facing the New York Stock Exchange. America's first government entered through the doors of St. Paul's Chapel, near Ground Zero, bowing down in prayer to consecrate the new nation's future into the hands of God. St. Paul's Chapel is near Ground Zero where, as a new nation, we committed to the Almighty. The Sycamore tree at Ground Zero shielded the Chapel from both the force of the implosion and the flying wreckage of the fallen towers.

The seventh harbinger: the Erez tree. After 9/11, the Sycamore tree, having been damaged beyond repair at Ground Zero, was uprooted and replaced with a pinacea tree where the Sycamore once stood. A ceremony was held around the tree and it, too, became a symbol entitled "the tree of hope" in defiance of God's judgment. Instead of turning themselves back to faith in God, the ancient Israeli people continued to place their faith in themselves and their own ability and resources to win a war with the Assyrians. In the same way here in America, our leaders gave a false hope built on nothing less than our own human efforts. We started a bold war with the descendants of the Assyrians in the Middle East, in the name of fighting terrorism, rather than returning to a belief in God and one of the main commandments, "Thou shalt not kill."

The eighth harbinger: the utterance. The eighth harbinger is the public speaking of the ancient vow of defiance. On September 11, 2004, vice presidential candidate John Edwards gave a speech in the capital city of Washington, DC, quoting Isaiah 9:10, word for word, without even realizing he was pronouncing judgment on America. Deceived by our own confidence in our corporate military complex, America followed a path that led to significant military, economic, social, and natural disorder. The rights of the American people became further eroded with the NSA spying on our own people, with many good Americans being thrown into prison as possible terrorists, due to the Patriot Act. No one made the connection between the chaos and our nation turning away from God.

The ninth harbinger: the prophecy. On September 12, 2001, the day after 9/11, America issued it's official response to the attack. The one in charge of issuing the response was Tom Daschle, Senate majority leader. As he closed his speech, he made a declaration – he proclaimed the ancient vow of defiance (Isaiah 9:10) before a joint session of Congress, word for word, to the world. At the end of the speech, he prophetically stated, "This is what we will do."

America found herself involved in a war on terrorism due to our own arrogance and active self-centeredness, and the defiance was a willful disobedience to God of heaven and earth, creator and sustainer of families, governments, and life itself.

In 2008, the military corporate complex and the bankers funding the "war on terrorism" found themselves in a financial crisis. Not only were they overpaying themselves, but they were also living their lives with prostitution and drugs, especially cocaine from South America, brought into America and sold to them by secret societies and

American drug lords, under the guise of the CIA. These clandestine operations further eroded the righteousness of the people of America, funding secret space programs and off-world operations, furthering the enslavement of the American people.

Barack Obama was elected president of the United States in 2008, officially bringing "change" to America, However, the same lawmakers of President Bush's term remained in power, and so this new American presidency continued with the enslavement of the American people. American health care, the fifth highest income producing bracket in the gross national product, was taken over by the government. The Executive Branch of government was only meant to execute the laws, properly voted upon by the representatives of the people in Congress. Executive orders, signed by the presidents of the corporate United States, were now becoming the law of the land without the consent of the people. The Constitution of the United States was further eroded and trampled upon.

The Judeo-Christian laws and statutes were put into place by the founding fathers at the start of our young nation, one nation under God. But that nation has become a nation of atheists, defying the laws of God and laws of its own constitution, which was made to protect freedom of all the citizens. We the people.

It is time to humble ourselves, like the founding fathers of this great nation, and ask for Divine Providence to assist us to return to freedom, and faith in the God of America, creator of the universe. It is time we again become a symbol of freedom to shine for all the world.

Chapter 33 - Father Gabriel's Parting Statements

I asked Father Gabriel to give me his thoughts when I departed. The words of wisdom he left me with were as follows:

"We live in one of the many moments, most interesting in the history of humanity, the awakening of human consciousness.

"It is not an economic crisis causing the problems on the planet. The crisis is a problem of values. Loss of spirituality and lack of transcending consciousness have produced humans who discard each other. Many of our children either die from abortion or end up in the streets because we have lost sight of the value of every human being.

"I learned the meditation techniques over 30 years ago. These techniques are an inspiration to my personal life and the work I perform. We work with thousands of children living in the streets. More than 30,000 Colombian children were put in the streets during the drug wars, which continue to this day. Through the Hogares Claret, we have worked with over 3500 of these children and young adults each year. Teaching Transcendental Meditation as a part of the rehabilitation of these children and the adults in the centers is of utmost value.

"Because of the meditation our centers have become centers of peace, humanity, and love. There is no violence, the children feel less stress, express happiness, the enjoyment of life is heightened, compassion is present and feelings of love transform each child like an imperial medicine removing all the negativity of past violence, sickness, and emotions of being discarded by their loved ones and families.

"We teach the children to overcome all the negative feelings which have been causing the problems in their lives and replace them with consciousness and feelings of love. By helping every aspect of their life to feel self-respect, self-love and self-introspection, they become a positive part of the community. We have many therapies of consciousness, using a connection to the earth, a connection to the plant world with gardening, connecting to the animal world with horse therapy, and connecting to other human beings through games and sports. We also incorporate the Boy Scouts for our male participants and the Girl Scouts for the female participants, with perfect institution of human cooperation.

"We will send bombs of love to the entire world!

"All of the programs of the Hogares Claret present these children and adolescents with the skills necessary to provide success in their lives. But more than that, we provide them with the emotional stability to evolve into productive and loving participants in the community.

"My job currently is to globalize love with programs of love consciousness and meditation, so that all of the children of Latin America and the world can learn to meditate and participate in the consciousness of love. This consciousness will change the world. "

—Father Gabriel

Father Gabriel Mejia

About the Author

Scott R. Werner originally began working in medicine as a practicing OB/GYN, but became a medical intuitive after curing his own cancer with herbs and healing energy. He gave up his medical practice to focus on the real causes of disease. He now lives in St. George, Utah, with his wife and children. Scott has used herbs, homeopathic & energetic remedies, Toning (God sounds) and natural detoxing to help improve and heal untreatable illnesses and dis-ease, helping thousands of clients. He offers intuitive medical spiritual readings for clients, putting them on the products that will help them the most. Scott currently lectures to many groups in Minnesota, Nevada, California, Iowa, Hawaii, Florida, Utah, South Dakota and Peru, teaching about herbal products, homeopathics, essential oils, energy and spiritual healing.

Connect with Scott:

Web – www.scottwerner.org

Facebook.com/TakeBackYourHealth.book

Email – scott.healthlongevityinc@gmail.com

Phone for Intuitive Readings – (435) 986-0025

Also by Scott Werner

Take Back Your Health
(Balboa Press, 2012)

Take Back Your Health was written as a sort of oracle book and has been tested by several intuitives to vibrate in unconditional love consciousness. It is meant to be opened where you are guided each day; the modality of healing for your body will be revealed.

- Clean up and detoxify your body.
- Revitalize your organs and brain function at the cellular level.
- Intuit for yourself what you should do each day for your health.

"I would open the book each day, and it was exactly what I needed. I am so impressed with the energy of each story. It has helped me so much."

—C. Larsen, Utah

"I was lying in my bed, sicker than I'd ever been in my life. I received a copy of your book and read the chapter on Happy. It was exactly what I needed to get me going again. Thank you, thank you, thank you."

—L. Ryan, New York

"Thank you, Scott. I cannot tell you how helpful the fear-facing chapter was. Today was literally a life-changing day for me."

—Lindsay de Swart, Canada

Also by Scott Werner

The Next Step in Human Evolution
(Health & Longevity, Inc., 2015)

Evolve Your DNA!

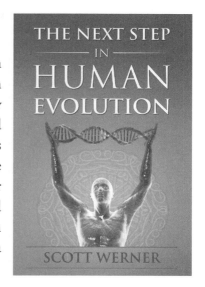

Industrial capitalists have created an environmental catastrophe through the use of toxic chemicals, heavy metals, radioactive pollutants, and even nano-robotic brain and nervous system control technologies. These contaminants have infiltrated our water sources, the air we breathe and our food, having a severe impact on the human race and our ability to live a normal, healthy life.

Due to this constant barrage of toxins, detoxing these contaminants from the body is no longer possible using conventional methods. Something greater is needed – something that could only be provided from a higher dimension – and Scott Werner has been given the answer. Appearing to Scott one night while traveling, St. Germaine presented a simple solution to our current polluted global condition.

"I come to you with an answer!" said St. Germaine. *"Evolution is the answer and is inevitable for survival on this beautiful planet. I will tell you how this is to be done."*

The Next Step in Human Evolution provides a way to evolve our DNA to be resistant to the toxic environment, inflammatory diseases, and degenerative brain and nerve conditions faced by the population today.